JOURNEYING WITH INDIA

JOURNEYING WITH INDIA

Reflections of the Inward Eye

MEMOIRS OF A CIVIL SERVANT

Y.N. Varma

SPEAKING
TIGER

SPEAKING TIGER BOOKS LLP
125A, Ground Floor, Shahpur Jat, near Asiad Village,
New Delhi 110049

First published by Speaking Tiger Books 2023

Copyright © Anupam Varma, Ashutosh Varma and Anshuman Varma

ISBN: 978-93-5447-486-6
eISBN: 978-93-5447-489-7

10 9 8 7 6 5 4 3 2 1

All rights reserved.
No part of this publication may be reproduced, transmitted, or stored in a retrieval system, in any form or by any means, electronic,
mechanical, photocopying, recording or otherwise,
without the prior permission of the publisher.

This book is sold subject to the condition that it shall not, by way of trade or otherwise, be lent, resold, hired out, or otherwise circulated, without the publisher's prior consent, in any form of binding or cover other
than that in which it is published.

PREFACE

The French writer Stéphane Mallarmé said, 'Everything in the world exists in order to end up as a book.' I am not sure my grandfather shared this belief entirely, but he did intend to publish his memoir, which he began writing in the mid-1970s, a few years after he retired from the civil service. He completed a first draft in 1981 and put it aside. Perhaps he intended to revise it, add more of his experiences and insights. We will never know. Fortunately, he kept the handwritten pages carefully and now, some forty years later, we, his family, have been able to put them together and publish this posthumous memoir.

We called him Bapu in the family. His friends and service colleagues called him Yogi. He was an affectionate father to his two sons, my father and my late Govind Chacha. To us, his grandchildren, he was the ever-caring, indulgent grandfather who pampered us, and did so much to secure our future in his inimitable style. He also had a deep connect with his nephews and nieces and others in the extended family, and some outside it, whom he influenced with his personality. He was as dear to them as they were to him. It was a reciprocal sense of belonging.

Bapu was a son of the soil, who by sheer grit and determination rose from humble beginnings in our native village, Katra, in the Bikapur tehsil of the erstwhile riyasat of Khapra Deeh, thirty-five kilometres from Faizabad/Ayodhya. He made it to the Provincial Civil Service of the United Provinces in 1936, thus becoming a part of the service that Sardar Patel was to describe as the 'steel frame' of India. For thirty-five years Bapu served his country and his people—through the upheavals of the Second World War, the heady days of the Quit India movement, the tragedy of Partition, the euphoria of Independence and free India's first elections, and then the excitement, challenges and high idealism of nation-building in the 1950s and '60s.

Bapu was a larger-than-life presence for us, like a large, sheltering tree in whose shade we flourished. It is a daunting task to sum up his personality. But there is an incident I remember from my childhood which I think is revealing. I was ten years old when I witnessed an exchange between Bapu and my father. The issue was about getting some young person in need of employment a government job, and Bapu broached it with my father, himself a member of the IAS. My father politely refused, citing the rule book. At this, Bapu smilingly retorted, '*Tum log naukri karte ho, humne baadshaahat ki hai.* (You people merely serve in the civil service, while in our time we were rulers.) I *wrote* the rule book!'

Throughout his career, Bapu was instrumental in getting jobs for a number of youngsters from his own and neighbouring villages. So much so that the village elders, he once told me, complained to him that he had denuded their villages of young blood. In retrospect, this may have made him sad as he looked back, but there was always a gleam in his eyes when he spoke about having carved out careers for many youngsters. He had made a difference in the lives of so many people, and that seems to have been what he was happiest about.

Apart from his official personage, in his personal life Bapu was deeply spiritual. His religious beliefs were what humane Hinduism is, and will always be. I had the good fortune of spending my childhood and my growing-up 'wonder' years with Bapu. I recall that during the fifteen days every year when devout Hindus observe pitra-paksha or shraadha (ancestor worship), just before the Navratri in September-October, he used to do 'tarpan'—an offering of water to all of one's ancestors. He would tell us that he also did tarpan to those departed souls he had known whose descendants would not or could not do this rite of passage. He used to do tarpan to every familiar deceased person who flashed upon his 'inward eye'— Maulvi Saheb, who taught him in school, his friends, mentors, and service colleagues who had left this world for the other. That was typical of Bapu.

Bapu was our window to knowledge and the world. A self-taught scholar of Sanskrit, he would keep us enthralled with his recitations of shlokas and hymns. As most grandparents would in those days, he narrated the epics *Ramayana* and *Mahabharata* to us, and also stories and ballads from folklore. I remember, especially, the tale of Alha and Udal, the brave twelfth-century warriors in the realm of the Chandela king Parmal of Mahoba. Even as I write this, I can hear Bapu recite the *Alha Khand* ballad:

> *Khat-khat khat-khat tega baaje, chhapak-chhapak baaje talwaar*
> *aur bahut ladaai kar ke bhi, Mahoba waalon se toh haar gayi talwaar...*

He was a treasure of memories of his time and the time preceding his generation, and would share numerous anecdotes with us. I still remember the thrilling shikar stories that he would tell us in vivid detail. We were to read these stories some years later in Jim Corbet's magnum opus, *Man-Eaters of Kumaon*, and the other books he wrote. For my siblings and me, our shared memories of those years are richer because we were blessed to have a grandfather like Bapu.

I learnt in Bapu's lap about our freedom struggle, our Constitutional history and the realities of post-Independence politics, all of which I actually read about only years later in textbooks in school and college and during my professional education. In his own way he skilled us for the life that was to be for us. The most precious gift that Bapu bestowed on us as a family was the treasure of a wide and eclectic knowledge, rich experience, fond memories, 'sanskaar' and good behaviour. He, along with 'Amma', my grandmother, inculcated in us a sense of empathy and compassion for those less fortunate. He gave us wisdom gained from his own insights, and his experiences as an administrator, to overcome life's challenges and rise above them. He groomed us for life, showing us what to expect from it—some good things, some middling and some not so good. Above all, he made us resilient.

For whatever, wherever we are as a family today, it is Bapu we need to thank God for. We live his dream. Although he would have been a tiny bit disappointed in me and my two younger brothers for not having made it to the civil services. But that was how it was to be.

I also had the good fortune of seeing Bapu write the original manuscript of this book sometime in the late 1970s on full-scape paper in his beautiful handwriting with long strokes. He would sit at his mahogany office desk and write for hours together, with just a table fan to provide relief from the heat and a comforting background hum. He would discuss with Amma, my Dadi, some of the portions he had written and if need be, he would re-work them. It would have been his earnest desire to have his memoir published. It is that wish which we as his descendants are now fulfilling as a sacred duty in the form of this book. We only wish we could have published it much earlier. But *'Der se aaye, par durust aaye'*, as Bapu would say.

We as a family continue to be shaped by Bapu's legacy, and in this context, this book is our gift to my father, Mr Arvind Varma. Bapu himself would have dedicated the book to his two mentors in service, Late Shri Shankar Prasad, ICS and Late Shri Aditya Nath Jha, ICS. At a personal level, he would have dedicated it to his father, Lala Rameshwar Prasad, to his wife and 'ardhaangini', Smt. Parvati Varma, and to his sons: my father, and my uncle, Late Mr. Govind Varma.

In fond remembrance of Bapu,

Anupam Varma
New Delhi, July 2023

JOURNEYING WITH INDIA
Reflections of the Inward Eye

INTRODUCTION

Ever since my retirement in 1971, I have been obsessed with the idea of writing my memoirs. My career encompassed fairly variegated times. I started service in the Provincial Civil Service (PCS) of the United Provinces (later, Uttar Pradesh) in 1936, during the heyday of the British Raj. At this time, I served in a number of districts reporting to various British Collectors till 1947. From 1937 to 1939, I had the privilege of working under the first Congress government. I was also part of the government effort during the Second World War. I was a witness to, and had to deal with administrative matters arising out of the national movement of the time, specially from 1940 to 1942. I also witnessed the great holocaust and exodus during India's Partition in 1947. After India won Independence, I was the Home Secretary in the then Delhi State from 1947 to 1954. It was a state with a population of around 9 lakh in 1949 but with a refugee issue that I had to handle. It was my privilege to have had a hand in the building up of Delhi's administration, the police force, and also in the construction of the Tis Hazari courts and Tihar Jail. Thereafter, I was in the Indian Airlines Corporation, from 1954 to 1958 in the initial stages, and worked out the rules, helped in establishing the headquarters, while merging the staff of different companies into an integrated Indian Airlines structure. I take pride in having been somewhat responsible for the construction of Airline House at Calcutta and Delhi.

I have functioned as Excise Commissioner of Uttar Pradesh (1958-61), as Agriculture Extension Commissioner in the Ministry of Food and Agriculture (1961-64), and also as Director General, All India Radio, and as Joint Secretary, Ministry of Information & Broadcasting (1964-68). I worked with Mrs Indira Gandhi from October 1964 to January 1966—an unforgettable experience.

With these rare and valuable understandings, I have been persuaded by friends to set forth in writing some of the important events that may be of interest to others. Though historians, academicians and politicians have given their versions of what transpired during the freedom movement in 1942, there does not exist a narrative of exactly what happened in 1942 from the viewpoint of a civil servant who witnessed many events up close. I have also given an account of the British Collectors—their intelligence and commitment and also their shortcomings. And so this peep into the past may be a peep into history as well.

What had dissuaded me so far from undertaking this journey was the futility of it. A record of experiences in life, as Macbeth said in the play, is just 'a tale told by an idiot, full of sound and fury, signifying nothing'. At best, it promises glimpses of a bygone age and has no more than a semi-historical value. But even histories are being re-written now, and the greatest are getting forgotten. To many, Gandhiji is just a name; and many other shining figures are fading into oblivion. The rush and speed of modern civilization is like an avalanche which is obliterating all pillars and pyramids of history.

And yet the urge to record what one has seen persists. When the river rushes on, the mountain stays and remembers. We like to remember and look back. And so is the case with this glimpse into the past.

Allahabad
1981

1

I was a student of the University of Allahabad from 1932 to 1936, where I lived in Muir Hostel. Perhaps it would be pertinent here to start with a description of the status and stature of the university at that time. Allahabad University was the most outstanding university in northern India then. No university, except perhaps Madras University and Bombay University, was considered equal to the reputation and merit of Allahabad.

A galaxy of eminent professors illuminated its halls and portals, the likes of whom no other university could boast of, barring a few great professors in south India and at Calcutta University. Just to name some, there were Dr Beni Prasad in the Department of Politics, Sir Shafaat Ahmad Khan with his brilliant Readers Dr Ishwari Prasad and Dr Ram Prasad Tripathi in the History Department, Dr P.K. Acharya assisted by Professor K.C. Chattopadhyay (later Vice Chancellor of Sanskrit University) and Dr Babu

Ram Saxena in the Sanskrit Department. There were also the legendary Professor Ranade in the Department of Philosophy, and the celebrated Professor Amarnath Jha assisted by erudite scholars like Professor S.C. Deb, Dr E. Dastoor and Professor Raghupati Sahai (Firaq). Dr Meghnad Saha taught there in the Physics Department and Dr N.R. Dhar in the Department of Chemistry.

The number of students was not more than 1200, and there was a strong bond between the gurus and disciples. Students had a reverence for the teachers, and the teachers had affection towards their students whom they would sometimes treat like their own children. It was not unusual for groups of students to go to the residences of their teachers where they were welcomed warmly. Professor Amarnath Jha was famous for his personal connect with his students, specially with those in Muir Hostel, of which he was the warden.

The university breathed an atmosphere of discipline and learning. Unemployment as it exists today was not there, and every student of the university could get some job somewhere. Hence an air of relaxed scholarship abounded here.

The hostel itself was an interesting place. There were no electric fans in most of the rooms here. In Muir Hostel not more than six students had fans. The normal dress we wore was shirt, pyjama and chappal. The mess charges did not exceed Rs 12 a month. Scandals were rare as there were no girl students at the Bachelor's level. There were only four girl students in M.A. Previous in the English Department in my time, and two in M.A. Final. Smt. Mahadevi Verma was the solitary woman in the Sanskrit Department. Yet wise guys hinted whisperingly at scandals only to enliven conversations and to add spice to their lives.

Muir Hostel had the best of students. This was because Professor Jha admitted those who obtained the top positions in the Intermediate Examination, as well as the best sportsmen, the sons of the great and the important, and also students brilliant in music or other fine arts. Meritorious students aspired to obtain admission in Muir Hostel. And hence top-notchers not only of this state, but from all over India tried to find a berth here. And thus Muir Hostel became the centre of learning and competition at that time.

The most important government services of the day were the Indian Civil Service (ICS) and the Provincial Civil Service (PCS). Not more than three posts were open for competition in the ICS and PCS each, one seat being reserved for a Muslim. The non-Muslims had to compete for two posts in the ICS at the all-India level, and for the PCS at the state level. The competitive examinations for these were held by the Federal Service Commission and the papers were the same except in the PCS the optionals were for 600 marks, whereas for the ICS it was 800.

All the students preparing for the civil service exams were concentrated in Muir Hostel. Since the hostel housed so many high achievers, Professor D. Ojha, superintendent of the hostel, took pride in declaring these words: 'India is northern India, northern India is Allahabad University and Allahabad University is Muir Hostel.'

During the years that I was in the hostel, many who went on to become luminaries in their fields were there as well. L.P. Singh, who was later Home Secretary and Governor of Assam Hill states; Shriman Narain, the great Gandhian and also Governor of Gujarat; S.K. Banerji, who was our Ambassador in many countries; Foreign Secretary B.D. Pande, who also served as Cabinet Secretary and Governor of West Bengal; P.N. Haksar, Secretary to Prime Minister, just to name a few. A number of others also subsequently became brilliant Indian Administrative Service and Indian Police Service officers, Commissioners, Secretaries to Government and Inspector Generals of Police, Vice Chancellors, and distinguished themselves in many other walks of life.

Here a mention has to be made of the political situation of the time. The British Empire was well rooted, and the authority of His Majesty held unflinching sway. Indiscipline or violation of norms was not tolerated. The student community, the public and the people at large accepted the status quo and the might of the British

Raj. The nationalist movements launched in 1930 and 1932 certainly caused ripples in the university and in the Government Intermediate College, but by and large, the students attended to their studies and continued to learn and study and aspire to high positions. In my time, one boy in the hostel was suspected to be a CID agent who conveyed information to the police about sedition, and so all the students avoided him.

Thus, around the university, life flowed tranquil. I recall the great inter-university debate in the Senate Hall in 1933, when Adityanath Jha, brilliant and smiling, conducted the debate as President of the Union. Boys spoke and competed in an atmosphere of great enthusiasm and acclaim. There was another time when Rabindranath Tagore, the Nobel prize-winner, visited. He sat on the dais in the Senate Hall, and all the professors sat at his feet. The Muslim boarding students boycotted this idolatry, but still could not resist the temptation of coming to see him. Another time, the Great Gama, the world-renowned wrestler, delivered a speech in the Muir Central College hall in 1934.

The Collector and the Commissioner of Allahabad were Englishmen. Gandhi and Nehru were famous by now and attracted many followers. The flame of patriotic sentiment had been lit, but the British Raj seemed forever enduring and unalterable. While some students donned khaddar and became openly nationalist and Congress supporters, the bulk of the students continued in their traditional ways, and life flowed placid and tranquil like the waters of the Yamuna at the Sangam. This then was the state of affairs in the university, when I left in 1936.

2

I sat for the ICS and PCS examinations in 1935, and was selected for the PCS. As I was barely twenty-two years of age, I got my appointment deferred so I could appear for the ICS examination again in 1936. I was not selected, so I stayed in the PCS and was appointed Deputy Collector at Hardoi (in Uttar Pradesh) on 1 July 1936.

I stayed at the house of Agha Mirza Saheb, a senior Deputy Collector and a friend of my father-in-law. Agha Mirza Saheb lived in an old and huge bungalow with a large compound, where there were around fifteen servants. Each servant got a salary of four to five rupees a month. Agha Mirza also had an apartment away from the main house where a Brahmin cook and kitchen were kept for his orthodox Hindu guests. When he was posted at Allahabad as Registrar, Board of Revenue, Agha Mirza Saheb had a boat and a panda (Brahmin priest) and would go to the confluence (Sangam) of the Ganga and Yamuna for a bath almost every morning. During this time, there was an atmosphere of communal harmony and understanding at all levels.

After joining, I called on the Collector, G.W.M. Whittle. He passed orders attaching me to senior officers for training, and also asked me to read Dr Panna Lal's *Guide to Junior Collectors*. He also asked me whether I had read the autobiography of Pandit Jawaharlal Nehru.

I should explain here the significance of these two books at the time. Dr Panna Lal's book gave guidance to officers on how to conduct themselves and also how to meet the landed gentry—the zamindars and taluqdars. The feudal system was well entrenched and big landowning zamindars and taluqdars were owners of whole villages and land that was cultivated by the peasantry. This institution was the main bulwark on which the British system of administration rested. It was more or less a continuance of the system from the time of the Mughals and the nawabs. So the zamindars had to be treated with courtesy and their position and dignity had to be recognized. At the same time, the Collector and his administration had to make sure that the subjects of His Majesty were not wronged or oppressed and hence the district administration needed to ensure justice amongst the people. Injustice and high-handedness were to be eliminated, so that while developmental work was not the objective, life in the traditional ways was not to be tampered with. Land revenue was the source of revenue of the province, there being no taxes like sales tax. Hence the revenue administration from the Collector to the Patwari had to be supervised strictly, and revenue offices had to ensure the correctness of records by doing field-to-field checks.

The District Magistrate, all his Deputy Collectors, and the police had to see that life was secure in the villages. Cases of burglary received great attention. Dacoity and robberies were rare, and murders sporadic. When the officers went to winter camps and rode on horseback, there was calm and peace reigning around the green fields and sleepy villages. The government servants moved about in an atmosphere of cool comfort, indulging in occasional shikar or bird-shootings.

G.W.M. Whittle's suggestion to read Jawaharlal Nehru's autobiography was due to a new angle that had opened up in the political situation of the time. The Indian National Congress was forging ahead. The civil disobedience movements of 1930 and 1932 had sent ripples in the villages, as well as among the intelligentsia in the cities. Khaddar-clad Congressmen were to be seen almost everywhere, and nationalist sentiment was high. Gandhiji's Dandi March had electrified the masses, as had Pandit Nehru's Lahore Declaration of 1929, demanding complete independence. The Englishmen could not fully understand Gandhiji with his philosophy of ahimsa and of religion mixed up with politics. But the Oxford-educated Pandit Nehru spoke in a language and with a rationale which was understood by the Englishmen. But I noticed that even in 1936, sycophants were not wanting amongst title-holding and landowning classes who assured the English Collector that the Congress crowd was a pack of hoodlums who would be ousted at the elections. I was one of the presiding officers in a village called Bharail, at the first provincial elections in February 1937 that were mandated under the Government of India Act of 1935. The Congress party scored a complete victory. All Indians rejoiced, including the Indian officers.

In this connection, I may mention the visit to Hardoi of the Premier Pandit Govind Ballabh Pant of the first Congress government that was formed in the United Provinces as a result of the election in 1937.

Since 1921, Home and General Administration were not transferred subjects to the Indian legislature. In 1937, the Indian Council of Ministers in the Province were in-charge of all subjects, including Home and Administration. It was the first visit of the Premier of the Indian Government in the United Provinces, belonging to the Indian National Congress. So, the Collector J.K. Coghill (G.W.M. Whittle had left for Allahabad as Collector), the four senior Deputy Collector Sub-Divisional Officers, and myself as extra-

Magistrate together with the Superintendent of Police (SP) and Deputy Superintendent (Deputy SP) lined up at the Hardoi railway station awaiting the arrival of the special train of the Chief Minister, or the Premier, as he was called then. There were great crowds of Congressmen from the rural areas. The English Collector, along with all of us, stood at a distance, not rubbing shoulders with the crowd. On alighting from the train, Pandit Govind Ballabh Pant was greeted and surrounded by the Congress workers and went to the Railway Rest House. There, we sat in the veranda, waiting to be summoned. Despite the inconvenience caused to us, we Indian officers felt a malicious delight in observing Mr Coghill fidgeting about in his chair and impatiently moving about, heartily disliking not being given the priority and the importance which as the Collector and an Englishman he was used to getting. While I agree that the Collector should have received priority as head of the district administration, without doubt we were pleased to watch him wait and squirm. At this time there was also a black flag demonstration by the militant wing of the Muslim League, led by Nawab Aijaz Rasul of Sandila.

Another incident relates to my visit to Shahabad tehsil. As a second-class magistrate, I became Sub-Divisional Magistrate (SDM), Shahabad for a month at the age of about twenty-four. As I rode to the outskirts, I was asked by the tehsildar to get down for a ceremony. A chair and a cot with a bedspread were laid out for me. I was told that I had to beat five men with my shoes! On my way back, I had to do the same to a set of another five men. It was explained to me that in this locality an officer had been assaulted in the near past, and since then this punitive action was taken whenever the SDM passed that way. As a young man fresh from the university, I could not continue the ceremony, and so I stopped it.

On travelling further towards the village of Pali, I came across the ruins of what would have been a village. It was explained to me that a Sub-Inspector of Police who had abused an old man had been done to death on the cot on which he was sitting under a tree, by the four sons of the enraged old man. Accordingly, the might of British administration went into full play. All the villagers were arrested, mercilessly beaten and tortured, prosecuted and sentenced to transportation for life in the Andamans. In addition, the village had been dug to its foundations, burnt and razed to the ground. No doubt, English might and authority reigned supreme those days.

J.K. Coghill was a rough officer with rude and forbidding manners. He, however, took a keen interest in my training. I had to see him every week and he set me tasks and examined the reports written by me. On my winter tour diary, he gave detailed instructions. After I had been in the district for one year, he called me and told me that he had given me the following annual entry: 'An intelligent and promising officer who thinks too much of himself.' Then he told me that Commissioner Harper had noted the following remarks: 'An officer at his age, to be at all useful later, must think too much of himself.' This is an example, one of many, of the forthright manner of English officers.

Another incident with J.K. Coghill is even more interesting. The Collector transferred to me a complaint case under section 325 of the IPC. I tried the case and acquitted the accused. I further called upon the complainant to show cause why he should not be fined for having lodged a false and frivolous complaint and fined him. This happened sometime in 1937. While camping at Sandi about 30 km from Hardoi, a month or so later, I received the case file and a page of typed comments on the case by Coghill. In it, he criticized my judgement and said that my conclusions were wrong. I was young and imbued with idealism, apart from being distrustful of the District Magistrate's interference with my judicial integrity. So, immediately, in my mood of righteous indignation, I wrote out my comments in detail, and also added that Mr Coghill appeared to be prejudiced because the case related to the father-in-law of the Collector's orderly Ram Bali. On enquiry I had found it a false complaint, and the police had accordingly taken no action on the FIR and that Mr Coghill was the last person to sit in judgement over my judicial finding. I wrote it, sealed the entire file, marked it confidential and sent it to him. On my return to Hardoi, I was summoned by Mr Coghill to his office in the afternoon. Then a little later he directed that I should see him the next day, which was a Sunday, at his residence at 10 a.m. Imagine a young Indian officer being called up by a rude District Magistrate, that too an Englishman. I felt this was the end of my career. Unlike other days, when I met him in his office, this time I was seated in his drawing room. I was there on time, and Coghill arrived as well. What he said surprised me no end. He wanted to apologize to me for what he had written, and said he wanted to shake hands! He assured me, however, that it was not a false case, but that the police had tampered with it.

This spirit of fairness characterized many of the British officers I worked under. Their word was as good as a written document. They also wholeheartedly supported us even if we went wrong sometimes, and had a lot of confidence in our judgement. All these were admirable qualities and are very rare these days.

My father-in-law, Mr Tarkeshwar Prasad, who was a member of the Board of Revenue, related to me another incident about the Collector of Hardoi from the 1920s. There was a Deputy Collector named Raj Bahadur Singh in Hardoi. The English Collector circulated a note to the effect that officers should write in a more legible hand. Raj Bahadur

Singh commented on the note that with his handwriting he had stood first in B.A. in Allahabad University and he would be unable to give up that handwriting. Then the note passed on to the Joint Magistrate who was an Englishman from the ICS. He commented that the remark appeared to be addressed to him but that with this handwriting he stood first in the ICS in London, and he refused to give up the handwriting.

When the circulated note reached the Collector, he obviously could not proceed against the English Joint Magistrate, but he called up Raj Bahadur Singh to his office, rebuked him and conveyed that he could be dismissed for this impertinence. Whereupon Raj Bahadur, who was also the Taluqdar of a state in Sitapur, submitted that in case he was dismissed, he would go back to his taluqdari, and if this Collector was ever posted to Sitapur he would have to, according to custom, call on him, but that in case the Collector was dismissed, he would make sure that he did not have even the money to pay his passage back to England. This infuriated the Collector so much that he rained abuses on Raj Bahadur Singh, who in turn, already incensed, beat the Collector with his shoes!

The matter was reported and the Commissioner, an Englishman, came to conduct an enquiry. As was the custom, he stayed with the Collector and called Raj Bahadur Singh to meet him. But Mr Singh was not one to give up.

He sent word that since the Commissioner was staying with the Collector, there was a question on his impartiality. The Commissioner had no choice but to move to the Railway Rest House. Here, both the parties were called and after both had had their say, both were transferred.

3

I learnt the ways of camp tours from my senior Nar Singh Narain with whom I was attached. At the time, I was about twenty-four years old, and my wife, Parvati, was around twenty. We had no responsibilities, and we moved about in villages and forests. I recall the lush green fields, the lazy atmosphere in the camp in the mango grove, the dust-laden roads along the villages, the short winter days, the still evenings and falling dusks, the fields, grounds and the simple sleepy hamlets. I can still see in my mind's eye the fresh lifegiving rays of the morning sun breaking forth as I stood ready to go on horseback for village rounds.

While posted at Hardoi, I failed the riding test at the departmental examination. So I was transferred to Lucknow for two months in January 1937, and attached to the 14th Hussars at the cantonment there. My trainer, a Major, was a rough Englishman who let me sit on the horse while it walked on the first day, then made me ride the horse at a trot the next day, and on the third day, took me along with twenty-nine other British men of the cavalry to the sand dune stretches of the river Gomati. I was sandwiched between the men, and after a walk and trot, the horses started galloping. Every minute I was in danger of falling and being crushed under the hooves, but they were all laughing and egging on my horse to go faster. The stupendous effort I put in to survive kept me balanced and that was the day I learnt riding. When a few days later, he made me jump hurdles, I got scared, fell and injured myself, at which the Major assured me that I should not be afraid as there was a hospital close by, and that, while training King Farooq of Egypt, he had broken one of the king's limbs.

After I had learnt all the tricks of the trade, he gave me free time to ride as per my sweet will. Every morning, I would take the horse and ride to the golf course, zoo and other open spaces, where my wife used to wait for me and I would show off my riding skills to her.

Riding those days had a meaning and purpose, as we had to visit villages in the interior on horseback. An officer on horseback commanded respect and also gained more intimate knowledge of all affairs in the sub-division or the district.

In Hardoi, I was also trained how to meet the big landowning zamindars. Every zamindar, according to his status, had to call upon the Sub-Divisional Officer (SDO) or the Collector in camp, and kept some silver rupees or gold coins on his right palm, with his left palm underneath when meeting the officer. The officer, as representative of His Majesty, had to nod and touch the money, which signified acceptance of the nazar, as it was called. I subsequently learnt that according to custom it was to be distributed amongst the orderlies.

It may be of interest to mention that the Collector and SDOs often went to court in shirt and shorts, and in winter in warm suits and ties. At dinner, decorum was maintained and official black European dress or black achkan with churidar and a cap was worn.

4

In July 1938, I was transferred and posted to Barabanki. The district is hardly 25 km from Lucknow and most of the officers got away to Lucknow every evening to a club or to relatives or for an evening in town. Here I must relate an incident told to me by Shanker Prasad, who was later Chief Commissioner of Delhi and Home Secretary, Government of India. He was posted here as a Joint Magistrate in 1930 or 1931, and used to go away to Lucknow to Mahomed Bagh Club. One day, the Indian ICS Collector of Barabanki (I am not naming him), who was also at the club, sternly asked Shanker Prasad whether he had obtained the Collector's permission in leaving the station (Barabanki). Shanker Prasad replied that he had not, but in future he would. In order to make an impression of his superiority, the Indian Collector then rebuked Shanker Prasad and insulted him. To this, the young and short-tempered Shanker Prasad reacted by slapping the Collector.

When this came to the knowledge of the government, the English Chief Secretary transferred Shanker Prasad to Moradabad where the dreaded M.H.B. Nethersole was the Collector, in order to iron out the ebullient irregularities of his personality. But the story does not end here. On reaching Moradabad, when Shanker Prasad called upon the Collector, Mr Nethersole looked at him and asked, 'Is it a fact that you gave a beating to your Collector? I wish I could do the same to my Commissioner.' Later, they got on famously.

The following incidents stand out prominently from my two years at Barabanki.

The Congress government had been elected in UP. The Governor, Sir Harry Haig, used to go out on tours and used to obtain first-hand knowledge from the Collector and Superintendent of Police about the functioning of the government, and how far they were interfering with the general administration. The Congress government had created a Rural Development Department and there was to be a Rural Development Officer in each district. As the government attached considerable importance to this work, instructions to the Collectors were that the most competent and senior Deputy Collectors should be given charge of the work. Even though I was the junior-most SDO with only two years of service, M.W. Abbasi, the Collector, designated me as Rural Development Officer.

When Pandit Govind Ballabh Pant, the Premier, visited Barabanki, and there was a tea party at which all the officers were present, he asked Abbasi who the Rural Development Officer was. I was produced before him. Now not only was I young, I looked like a high school student. Pandit Pant with his impressive stature looked down on me. Realizing what was going on in the Premier's mind, Abbasi waxed eloquent in my praise as a most competent officer with plenty of initiative, and fully justified why he had appointed one so young-looking to this post. Pandit Pant then looked at me and asked me whether the people in the villages believed I was the Deputy Collector. He directed me to always have both my orderlies alongside, wherever I went, to ensure that I was accepted as an officer.

Those days officers were held in esteem and the Collectors represented the authority of the British government. The attitude of the government was to absolutely trust the man on the spot. This did lead to vagaries in individual cases. For example, in Barabanki, M.W. Abbasi rarely went to winter camp, the prescribed period being three months for the Collector. But the Collector's tents moved from camp to camp according to the circulated schedule. But he was also the son-in-law of Justice Niamatullah, and the militant Muslim League supported the Muslim officers in general.

Another incident relates to my winter camp in

Haidargarh tehsil in 1938. The tour of the SDO used to be like this: There were two Swiss cottages lent to the SDO, one for court work and the other as his living quarters. In addition there would be a number of smaller tents for the camp staff. The grove in which they used to be pitched would be big mango groves, cleaned a day before by the tehsil staff. The camps were always crowded with policemen on duty, Naib Tehsildar, the court of wards officers, and some other petty village officials and henchmen. When the camp broke for the next halt, one tent and kitchen would be carried on a bullock cart to the next camp at night; the Collector or the SDO would find one set pitched at the next camp by the time he arrived by car or on horseback.

In one such camp, I, along with my wife, arrived at around 11 a.m. I noticed that a large retinue of men carrying huge baskets on their heads led by a supervisor were walking in a file towards the tent of the Peshkar or reader. My old Muslim orderly came up to me, saluted me and informed that the zamindar or landlord of the area, Thakur so and so, had sent foodstocks. I asked him to give the zamindar saheb my compliments and tell him that I had my food rations with me and so I did not need all that. In case I fell short of anything, I would certainly call upon him. The old orderly who had been many years in the service and who knew better, stood silently, obviously nonplussed. I, however, told him to convey what I had told him. After about half an hour or so, he came back and informed me that the zamindar wanted to pay his respects. I asked him to bring him along. The Rajput zamindar was about six feet tall, robust and well built, and clad in the court dress, i.e, in costly sherwani, churidar, appropriate socks and shoes, with a turban on which he flaunted a feather-like jewel, such as maharajas put on, and wore all his medals, while a sword hung by his side. He looked like a Rajput prince, of a noble and haughty mien, overall an impressive personality. He towered over my five feet three inches and student-like appearance. After presenting the customary coins on his palm which I touched with my hand, he straightened and asked me whether it was a fact that the huzoor (myself) had refused to accept the foodstuff and presents he had sent. I replied I had not rejected them, but as I had all the things the kitchen needed, I had merely meant that I would call upon his hospitality if I needed anything. The zamindar then changed his tone. I should not do jugglery with words, he warned, instead I should frankly admit that I had rejected his offerings.

By now he was in full flow. He would raise a rebellion in the locality, he warned, and as I was the Ruler's representative (hakim), and a Magistrate, I was free to arrest him. He would provide bullock carts, and my camp must shift from that grove and his area. Never before in his life he had been so insulted and humiliated, he fumed.

In that very grove, the Mughal governors had camped, and the Governor, the Commissioners and the Collectors, Superintendents of Police and SDOs. Always, without exception, according to the extent and quality laid down in his books of customs (wajibularz), he and his ancestors had sent food and presents to each dignitary for 200 years! Never before had anyone humiliated him and his ancestors thus. Given this insult, it was no longer possible for him to live in that locality, he would abandon it. But before doing so he was going to go to Barabanki to meet the Collector and convey to him how he had been humiliated and that he would send telegrams to the Commissioner and the Governor to that effect.

Horrified and overwhelmed, I asked Thakur saheb not to take the matter that seriously, and if he felt so injured, by all means I accepted all his foodstuff and presents. Finally placated, he departed.

Since then I introduced a procedure, where if any presents were received from the zamindar, I would take a handful from all the baskets thereby signifying acceptance, and the rest would be distributed among the staff in camp. It may also be mentioned here that these zamindars of the old nobility did not have any axe to grind nor did they expect any favour on this account. It was a custom, handed down from centuries, that representatives had to be treated with respect and should be properly looked after by the landowning tributaries. It is so unlike the present-day dinners or hospitalities by businessmen where there is always the underlying motive of gain.

As mentioned earlier, land revenue was the mainstay of the government, and the entire revenue staff had to safeguard it. It was the responsibility of the SDO to see if there was any concealment of rent on the part of the zamindars. While doing partal or spot-checking, the khasra entries in village fields, I discovered that the actual rent paid by the tenants in a few villages of Raja of Jahangirabad was more than the rent recorded in the papers. I accordingly made a report to the Collector for a fresh settlement of these villages. The Collector's house in Barabanki belonged to, and according to custom, was maintained by the maharaja, and so I came in for an adverse entry into my character roll in 1939, with a comment of 'Anti-zamindar'. It stuck to me. In 1941, when I applied for the post of Assistant Settlement Officer, the then member, Board of Revenue, Mr Shireff called me for an interview and asked for my assurance that I was no longer anti-zamindar. The maintenance of the zamindar and his dignity was one of the pillars of British imperialism and authority.

Another incident took place during my winter tour in 1939. I was SDO, Haidargarh, and camping at Trivediganj, which was about 8 km from Tehsil Haidargarh. Deputy Commissioner Abbase came to camp at the tehsil. In the afternoon around 2 p.m., I rode to the tehsil, had a meeting with the Deputy Commissioner and then mounted my horse for the return journey at around 4 or 5 p.m. Seated on the horse, in a tone of authority, I instructed the assembled crowd of the tehsil staff to look after the Deputy Commissioner well, and, having said so, galloped off in full view of the admiring staff. When I had ridden about half a mile, I noticed that the horse was getting out of control. All my efforts to control it with the reins proved fruitless. While tightening the reins, I noticed that the left rope had a knot, and so I urged the horse on to the right. It galloped below an overhanging mango branch. I ducked in order to avoid hitting my head on the branch, and in doing so, I fell down on the dusty road. The horse stopped for a while, and then galloped off towards the camp.

I was in khaki coat and breaches and covered in dust from head to foot. I had covered about a mile only and Trivediganj was some kilometres away. So I walked alone in the dust cloud raised by the galloping horse. I passed Kanwa village and one or two more villages. The entire crowd of village children came up, pointing at me with great glee as the person whose horse had run away. Amidst the shouts of these gleeful urchins, I walked along as the shadows lengthened. A patwari and kanungo came up from behind on their cycles, saluted me and offered me their cycles which I declined in a dignified manner and said I preferred to walk. They followed me on foot. Then I came across some villagers who had cut the road to take water from a well or pond to their fields across the road. During my onward ride to Haidargarh tehsil, I had threatened them and asked them to appear in court the next day. These road-cutters now assured me that their best efforts to detain the horse had failed. I obliged and told them that now they were not to appear in court and had been forgiven.

And thus I made my way, dust-laden, followed by the two revenue officials, and a platoon of gleeful children giving vent to their mirth in witnessing the fallen horseman jogging along. I can still close my eyes and see the gold and copper in the evening sky melting into the darkening horizon, as the soft stillness of the evening enveloped the fields. Finally the darkness lay like a pencil line above the treetops in the distant western sky. As I neared the camp, the evening star was shining in the sky.

Parvati, my wife, alarmed and frightened, accompanied by the camp people, met me about two furlongs from the camp. On reaching the camp grove, the ziladar of the court of wards, a polished and cultured Muslim, along with the remaining anxious-looking crowd enquired about my fall and whether I had been hurt. I narrated how I had fallen, and seeing my embarrassment, the ziladar assured me that it is only the brave amongst horsemen who fall. Later, as I took tea inside the tent with my wife, I could hear my peshkar Iduz Zafar shouting out to the horses' syce that my fall could be ascribed to no other reason but the faulty reins, and hence the entire responsibility for my fall was his, and his alone. This was followed by sounds of suppressed laughter.

Thus life went on in camps full of fun and plenty. Not less than a maund (1 maund=37.3 kg) of milk flowed into the camp. In the evening and at night in these wintry months, campfires were lit at different places because there was no dearth of wood, whole dry trees having been felled for camp use.

Amidst this atmosphere of peace and serenity, the camps of SDOs and Collectors functioned. Fires crackled as darkness spread around, and we went to sleep in white tent cottages, set amidst the gloaming darkness of the mango grove and the surrounding fields with their winter crops.

In September 1939, World War II broke out. England declared war on Germany as English warships were sunk off the Baltic Sea. I recall Dr K.N. Katju, a UP cabinet minister, coming to Barabanki soon after and in the public meeting held mentioning how a parting of ways was forthcoming, and the future was unpredictable. Soon after, the Congress government resigned, unable to offer cooperation to the British government in the operation of the war.

5

In April 1940, I arrived in Pilibhit on transfer from Barabanki and was there till 24 August 1942. The British government was at war and the main effort in the district was to see that the recruitment of men for the armies and the collection of war fund was not impeded. The Air Raid Precautions (ARP) organization was also set up, and I was the ARP Officer dividing the city into ARP units and training the public in air raid precautions—in which no member of the public was interested. War funds were collected from each tenant, well-to-do zamindars and businessmen. The normal work of the district administration, namely revenue work, and enforcement of law and order, however, continued as usual. The Muslim League, which had cooperated with the British government in the war effort, was taking more and more of a militant attitude and fomenting communal tensions in Pilibhit, where the proportion of Hindu and Muslim population was almost equal. I was SDO, Bilaspur and later SDO, Pilibhit and Puranpur tehsils.

In 1940, Gandhiji issued directions for offering individual civil disobedience. I found that the Congress MLAs who had enjoyed positions of power and importance in the district were not very enthusiastic about it. But as old Congressmen they had no option. One of them, Mukund Lal Aggarwal, was a most respectable man of good culture. He was also on good terms with me before he resigned as Chairman of the Rural Development Committee of the district. He asked me to help him by merely sentencing him to imprisonment and not fining him as the fine would be recovered from his family assets. So by arrangement he offered individual civil disobedience in front of a Bilaspur tehsil thana, and I arrived there in time to arrest him and sentence him for a term of six months. I then took him in my car, along with his luggage, and handed him over to the Superintendent of Jail. In each tehsil, such a case was repeated. Gandhiji, who always had a knack of feeling the pulse, was experimenting to gauge the extent of public opinion.

I felt there was no effect on the masses who continued to till their land as usual, and contributed their allotted share of war fund to the patwari. But I noticed a growing dissatisfaction with the helplessness with which we watched the conduct of the war. The feeling of being tied unwillingly to the bandwagon of the British was growing. At the same time, the arrogance and a sense of superiority among the officers was leading to hostility in the Indian officers, including those of the ICS. But Pilibhit was an out-of-the-way district, at the foothills of the Himalyas, and so life went on here. In May 1940, however, when France fell to Germany, the District Magistrate R.P. Bhargava took immediate precautions. Even in Pilibhit there was a sudden feeling that the Empire was about to collapse and that the Government of India might also collapse leading to large-scale lawlessness. So, Mr Bhargava managed to store large quantities of ammunition in the malkhana, and drew up a scheme to defend the town and the treasury. The sense that a collapse was at hand had gripped everybody. It is in this context that one can appreciate the famous speech of Winston Churchill, on the fall of France, which revived confidence once more.

Another important incident was the visit of M.H.B. Nethersole, the Commissioner of Bareilly, on 16 January 1942. Before I narrate that, it would be interesting to mention several incidents pertaining to this most dreaded and colourful ICS officer, some of which he related himself, at the Pilibhit club in the course of that visit.

One of the incidents was from when he was Collector at Pilibhit. It was his habit to ride a few miles every morning and on one such ride, he noticed a Kurk Amin (an official charged with carrying out a court's orders in the matter of properties). The official was attaching the goods of a house following a civil decree from a court. An old woman, whose house it was, was crying loudly. Nethersole rode up and directed the Kurk Amin to stop his work. The official, taking it as the vagary of the English Collector, went away, but came back the next morning to finish the work. Now Nethersole also had a hunch that the Kurk Amin would come back so he rode up again and found the operations on. This infuriated Nethersole, who went on to give a thrashing to the official with his cane and almost broke his limbs, and cautioned that in case he came again to do the kurki, he would be shot.

The Kurk Amin reported the matter to the District Judge of Bareilly who was also an Englishman. On the District Judge's cautioning Nethersole that his action constituted contempt of court and was punishable for obstruction of a judicial process, Nethersole wrote to him that he did not mind being prosecuted, but in case the amin went there again, he would surely shoot him. I was told the matter was dropped.

Another incident relating to him was mentioned to me by my father-in-law, Mr Tarkeshwar Prasad, who was a Deputy Collector in District Badaun when Nethersole was the Collector. One morning, when Nethersole was on a ride out of Badaun, he found a chowkidar hurrying towards the thana (police station) with some red envelopes in his hand. These envelopes usually carried information about serious crimes. Nethersole asked the chowkidar what the matter was, and was told that a communal riot was taking place in a village a mile away. He told the chowkidar to hurry on to the thana, and himself turned his horse in the direction of the village.

When he reached, he found that Hindu and Muslim villagers had gathered by the village pond, which was quite deep, and were fighting with each other. He stood for a while watching, and then in a swift move, caught hold of an old maulvi and jumped into the deep pond with him! Nethersole was about six feet tall, whereas the maulvi with his long beard was only five feet. The water was neck deep for Nethersole and he held the maulvi down into the water till the poor man was spluttering for air. All the while, he demanded to know why the maulvi had caused all this rioting. When the maulvi denied all responsibility, he pressed his head down again into the pond. This he did again and again, till the maulvi was half dead and till he had confessed and promised not to do so again. Meanwhile, all the Hindus and Muslims who were watching this tamasha stopped their rioting and begged Mr Nethersole to release the maulvi. Satisfied at this outcome, the Collector then rode back, and informed the police contingent rushing there to go back, as the rioting was over.

There are a few more incidents relating to Nethersole. Once he was going on tour on horseback, followed by a corpulent Naib Tehsildar also on horseback. This Naib Tehsildar had to be physically lifted on to the back of the horse because of his girth. On this day, Nethersole was riding absent-mindedly and came below an overhanging branch and fell down. The horse stopped. Meanwhile, the Naib Tehsildar came along, and being unable to get down, enquired from his seat in the saddle whether the saheb was hurt. This naturally exasperated Nethersole who stood up, swore at the Naib Tehsildar and pulled him down. Then he mounted his own horse, and rode away. The Naib Tehsildar, unable to get on the saddle, walked on foot, bridle in hand. After covering some distance, Nethersole looked back and sighted the poor man jogging along on foot. He understood the whole situation, and came back, and physically lifted the Naib Tehsildar into the saddle once more.

Yet another incident relates to when he was District Magistrate of Agra. This was related by him in my presence at the Pilibhit Club, when as city magistrate, I was having some trouble with the Muharram processions in the city. In Agra it was customary to lift the telephone wires as the height of some of the tazias exceeded 29 feet on the procession route. Nethersole felt that it was not proper to do so. So he called all the taziadars to the kotwali, and asked how many had tazias which were more than 29 feet high. About half a dozen hands went up. He then called up the nearest taziadar, lifted him up with his massive hands and fell to beating him mercilessly with his cane, till the taziadar shouted that he had uttered nineteen and not twenty-nine. Nethersole then invited the other taziadars to come out and tell without any fear, if anybody else's tazia was over 29 feet. No hands went up. He then asked his Reader to record that no tazias were over 29 feet in height and the signatures of all the taziadars were taken.

He had another story about tazias from when he was Deputy Commissioner, Faizabad. There was a peepul tree along the route of the tazias, one branch of which was very low. The Muslims wanted it chopped, while the Hindus were sensitive to any cutting of a peepul tree. This led to communal tension every Muharram. So one morning, Nethersole rode along that route, and beneath the overhanging branch managed to hit his head and fell down, swearing at the tree. A crowd collected. As the English Collector had been hurt, the Hindus immediately agreed to lop off the offending branch.

When Nethersole was Collector, Moradabad, the files sent to him by the office had accumulated and his stenographer was being pestered by the office superintendent to have the files cleared. Nethersole hated office work, and had paid no attention when his stenographer tried to put up the files. This happened for several days. One day the stenographer again asked Nethersole to kindly sign the files. Being in a foul mood, he took out his ruler (a small stick) and ran at the stenographer and threw the ruler at him. It missed him and the man ran out into the compound and hid in the bushes. A Rai Bahadur who had spotted the stenographer cowering in the bushes, went to see Nethersole, and was asked whether he had seen this scoundrel of a stenographer around. Rai Bahadur Saheb wisely said he had not seen him and asked what was the matter. Nethersole informed him that the fellow had been pestering him too much about files. In the heyday of the British Raj in India, such vagaries from the ruling class were not infrequent.

In another case, a Naib Tehsildar sought an interview with him when he was Commissioner at Bareilly. The Naib Tehsildar submitted that when Nethersole was Collector at Bareilly, he had given him an annual performance entry to this effect: 'He is a very good Naib Tehsildar, but he is the brother of so and so who is a bad man.' The Naib Tehsildar said that he had not been promoted all these years on account of this adverse entry. So Nethersole called forth the character roll, cancelled his remarks and wrote, 'When I made this entry I was young and very foolish. He is a very good Naib Tehsildar.'

Now this M.H.B. Nethersole, dreaded by officers, was on his winter visit to Pilibhit on 16 January 1942. His tents were pitched in the compound of the Collector, and I as City Magistrate was in charge of arrangements. All the SDOs had cleared up arrears, and had done all the inspections and were up to date in their work, lest Nethersole might choose to examine an item.

On 16 January 1942, 10.30 a.m. was the time fixed for Nethersole's interview of the officers. My turn came at 11 a.m. I bade him good morning and was asked to be seated. He then asked me, 'What are you?' I told him that I was SDO Pilibhit and Puranpur, and also the District Census Officer, Rural Development Officer, ARP Officer, ex-officio Chairman Cane Cooperative Society, and a few more things. He then told me that I was good for nothing and thoroughly useless and asked what had been the extent of rainfall the previous night. I still remember telling him it was 1.63 inches at Pilibhit. He then asked me what was the rainfall of Puranpur tehsil, which was 41 km away. I confessed I had not received the report on that yet. At this he repeated that I was good for nothing and useless. I kept quiet. His next question was the exact figures of land revenue collection. I gave the figures immediately. He commented that he was surprised, then asked the figures of canal dues collection. This I said I could not give in exact figures. So he went back to saying I was completely useless. In order to somehow acquire a foothold in his favour, I told him that my father-in-law, Mr Tarkeshwar Prasad, had had the honour of working under him. He was delighted at this mention, and immediately said that Mr Tarkeshwar Prasad was a first-class officer in the same measure as I was a useless officer.

When he found me completely demoralized, he gave me the following advice. He said that I was merely an SDO and SDM and when asked I should not have given the long list of other appendages. He advised me to tour every village in my tehsil, know all the good and bad men, as well as the names of every patwari, headman and lambardar. The next time he met me, he expected me to be better informed. In profound relief I came away.

Around noon that day, it was the turn of non-officials. Quite a crowd had collected to meet him, as Nethersole had been Collector at Pilibhit earlier. Khan Bahadur Hafiz Abdul Jalil was called. Before going in, he took my consent to his inviting Nethersole for dinner. When Khan Bahadur Saheb reached the office in the tent, this is what transpired as told by him and witnessed by me from outside. Without offering a seat, Nethersole asked him what his name was. Khan Bahadur mentioned it. Nethersole then looked up the visitor's register, and found that it had been somebody else's turn to be called then. Nethersole demanded to know how he had come when it was not his turn. Khan Bahadur Saheb remined him that he had been appointed honorary magistrate by Nethersole in his time as Collector. Nethersole said, 'damn honorary magistrate', but how had he come when it was not his turn. Khan Bahadur now said that he had been made Khan Bahadur in his time, and that he had come to invite him to dinner. Nethersole again burst forth, 'damn dinner' but how had he come. Absolutely nonplussed, the Khan Bahadur mentioned that he had been called by the orderly. So Nethersole called out for the orderly, and on his arrival, chased him away from the tent and threw the register at him.

He then returned, took his seat, and asked Khan Bahadur Saheb again how he had come. Now the Khan Bahadur took out notes for Rs 50 and said that he had come merely to pay Rs 50 towards the war fund. Nethersole accepted this and said the receipt would follow. And thus the interview was over. But the calculated effect of Nethersole's action and conduct was that the crowd of visitors, mostly sycophants, melted away completely.

In some time, I, too, learnt how to handle the more difficult situations that arose in my areas, however I never used such unorthodox methods as Mr Nethersole. There was one Thakur Puttoo Singh of Bamrauli in Bisalpur tehsil of Pilibhit. He was a notorious revenue defaulter, and a village terror who would beat up anyone who would cross him. In the last week of September 1940, I received a note from the Tehsildar while I was in court that Thakur Puttoo Singh, the notorious defaulter, would be present in court in a case and the opportunity should be taken to arrest him for default of revenue. Puttoo Singh was a hefty Thakur, well-built and tall. In court, I asked him whether he had paid up his revenue. He said he would, but as he had the reputation of being an incorrigible defaulter and a liar at that, I asked two police constables to handcuff him. As he was being taken, he requested the constables to let him have a word with me. Then he told me in a most beseeching and earnest language that his forefathers had a castle in Bamrauli and that his ancestors had maintained an army and they were rulers over a large number of villages. Nobody in the family had ever been handcuffed and gone to jail and that his family honour was at stake now. Would he pay the Rs 250 that was due, I asked him. The day was Friday, and he said he would do so on Tuesday. I released him and told him that in case he did not pay the dues on Tuesday, I would pay it as a fine for trusting him. He turned up on Tuesday and paid up. Then he told me that he was unable to stand the disrespectful attitude of his erstwhile subjects, which was why he would beat them up. I pointed out to him that it was his fault that he had lost all his property, and was in debt and he must forswear violence, else I would be compelled to take action against him. He promised upon the words of a Thakur. And during my stay, there were no more complaints.

Between 1940 and 1942, the discontent with British rule grew rapidly. The nationalist sentiment was strong.

The realization of the war funds from each tenant and villager gave rise to much resentment in the villages. The arrest, trial, and incarceration of Jawaharlal Nehru for four years by Mr Moss at Gorakhpur sent waves of anger, and enhanced the sense of humiliation and frustration amongst all classes, including the government servants who did their duties like hired mercenaries. Only the Muslim League stuck with the British, more as a counter to the Congress than otherwise. The foreign domination and British arrogance was as galling to most Muslims as it was to the Hindus.

In the War, the British were facing some reverses, but their propaganda published it as otherwise and glorified the advances made by the British forces. The few who had radios, tuned in secretly to the Berlin broadcast or the broadcast of Subhash Chandra Bose from the Far East.

In educational institutions, students sang forbidden patriotic songs and said 'Vande Matram', though undercover and with restraint. The local Ayurveda College, which had grown-up students, had become a centre of suppressed sentiments of sedition. One student, Dayanidhi Sharma, who wrote and recited fiery patriotic poetry used to be a frequent visitor to my house when I was City Magistrate, and within closed doors used to recite these beautiful and inflammatory songs and poems. A seething discontent and crippling helplessness had seized the people when Gandhiji gave the Quit India call on 8 August 1942.

Meanwhile, before August 1942, the Governor Sir Maurice Hallett was on the move and also visited Pilibhit. The administration was being geared to be more rough and severe, and to allow no quarter to nationalist sentiments or to the elements thwarting the war effort.

After 8 August, as the clouds hung black and menacing in the sky, the aftereffects of the Quit India resolution began. A list of persons to be arrested had already been drawn up and most of them were picked up during the night and lodged in jail. My favourite, Dayanidhi Sharma, the poet and student of Ayurveda College, was also among them. I put him in hiding in one of the outlying places and asked him to accompany me to Lucknow on August 24, as I was under orders of transfer to Gorakhpur. Later, I carried this boy with me in my compartment to Lucknow. Afterwards, he wrote to me from Joshi's Hospital in Delhi under the name of Kripanidhi Sharma asking for some financial assistance.

On the morning of 10 August 1942, we were all on the alert for possible repercussions. Meetings and processions had been banned. Arrests were still continuing. On 13 August, a small procession of some young boys was taken out. The civil guard, a force of amateur young men, had been constituted by the government in each district and they had been given grey shirts, shorts and lathis, and assigned duties to assist the police when so required. These civil guards stopped the procession, and when provoked, they attacked with their lathis. They hit one young Baniya boy on the head who died on the spot. The boy was hardly eighteen or nineteen, and had been married only six months earlier. The action was wholly unwarranted and unauthorized, but quite in line with the bulldog tenacity and severe attitude of the administration towards any nationalist expression.

This incident sent a wave of consternation in the public. On the 13th, the relatives made an application to the District Magistrate, Raghubir Singh, to take the dead body in a procession, which was refused. Later, on the intervention of some citizens, permission was accorded to take the body outside the city towards Deoha river where they could carry out the funeral procession.

On 14 August, the police were all on duty. I was on duty at the tehsil headquarters in the heart of the town. The city wore a sombre look and felt sinister and hostile. I prided myself on being a popular City Magistrate, but that day I felt like an agent of the British administration. I was amongst people who were not very friendly. The funeral procession became a crowd after it had passed the tehsil and I placed my car behind the procession to ensure that my presence prevented any untoward incident. The young widow of the boy was in a horse-drawn tonga, lamenting aloud, being supported by elderly women. All the respectable gentry and city people were following on foot, heads down. They saw that I was there, following the procession. By the time they reached the side of the Deoha river, the crowd could not have been less than ten thousand. I parked my car along the railway track, and stood watching, while the people descended below the bridge towards the riverbank, and moved towards the burning ghat near the waters. Evening had fallen, darkness was descending and the crowd near the burning pyre was mingling into shadows. It was around 7.30 p.m. by the time the pyre was lighted, and I saw flames leaping up into the darkness. I kept standing and watching. Then, suddenly, I noticed a movement. Along the Deoha railway track on the bridge, people were coming up, and once they took a look at me, they were trying to run away. I saw whole groups breaking away and trying to run away on seeing me. I also noticed that a railway engine passed the bridge on its way to Pilibhit station, and the driver looked out and saluted me without speaking. All this surprised me, but I sensed nothing very special.

Around 8.30 p.m., I came to my residence at the Collectorate about 4 km from the city. As I was undressing, I received a telephone message that the District Magistrate and the Superintendent of Police wanted me at the kotwali as a constable had been murdered at Deoha river bridge and the body thrown into the river.

After a hurried consultation at the kotwali and at the District Magistrate's house, Commissioner Barlow was telephoned around 9.30 p.m. Barlow had the reputation of being a rude man. He was perhaps tipsy and not pleased at having been telephoned at that hour. He expressed his displeasure at only one constable and a few civic guards having been posted at that end of the bridge, enjoined that strict action be taken and promised to send a company of armed police which would arrive during the night.

In the morning I was again on duty at the tehsil and police vigilance was stepped up. There were orders that no hartal should be allowed and no shops could be closed. Action had to be taken under the Defence of India rules. I made a round of the shops around 11 a.m. and found that some shops were not open. I got a squad to break open the locks and open the shops and confiscate goods. On my second round, all the shops were open except one. I directed that the shop be opened by force, and the owner and shopkeeper taken into custody under Defence of India rules. Meanwhile the man arrived, the shop was opened, but I arrested and sent him to jail. I directed the Kotwal to obtain a warrant of arrest later.

Later, the kotwali sent to me a number of warrants to be signed for complicity in the murder of the constable. The warrant of this businessman had been made out not under Defence of India rules, but for murder. I discovered that many wealthy businessman had similarly been arrested for the murder, and the warrants sent to me for signature.

On 15 August 1942, I expressed my apprehension to the District Magistrate Raghubir Singh that men of the business community were being arrested in order to extort money before releasing them, and that the actual perpetrators of the crime were goondas who could use swords and knives with which they had cut up the constable. Raghubir Singh agreed and directed me to record the statements of the eyewitnesses immediately to prevent large-scale persecution of the business community. I recorded these statements in the tehsil court. The eyewitnesses were mainly the civic guards and they named about fourteen persons. I handed over these statements in an envelope to Raghubir Singh and left on transfer to Gorakhpur on 24 August 1942.

In 1943, when I was posted at Gorakhpur, I came to know that the case, in which about fifty-two persons had been prosecuted, had acquired a serious dimension as Raghubir Singh had denied in the court of the District Judge that any statements had been recorded by me, and further that such statements did not exist. A commission was sent to a local magistrate of Gorakhpur to record my statement.

On the day of hearing of the case, Bihari Lal, government Pleader of Pilibhit, came to my house at 9 a.m., and showed me the statements recorded by me, and requested me on behalf of Raghubir Singh and T.S. Negi, SP, to destroy these and say that no such statements had been recorded by me. I used my sense, and promised to consider it, but that he should keep the statements with himself, lest it be alleged that I had brought the statements with myself and that they were in my possession.

In the court, on examination, I stated that I had recorded the statements and had left them with the Collector on leaving the district, and also that I had seen the statements with the government Pleader that morning. The statements were with him and he should be asked to deposit them in court. On the court's direction, he filed the papers, to my great relief. The case was transferred from Pilibhit to Moradabad in the court of Mr Chandramani, the District Judge. I was summoned as a witness against the government and was cross examined for two hours and had to answer the allegation that since I was anti-British and had Congress leanings, I had recorded the statements on my own and that I had left the papers in a way so that the DM had no knowledge. The case ultimately ended in acquittal.

Soon after, I received a threatening message from Raghubir Singh saying he would report me and seek my suspension and dismissal. I immediately went to Mr I.U. Alexander, the District Magistrate of Gorakhpur, and narrated to him the whole story. The English District Magistrates were already satisfied with my handling of the 1942 disturbances at Bhatani on the border of UP and

Bihar, and conveyed to Raghubir Singh that any report against me to the government would be at his peril. And so the matter ended.

Pilibhit public opinion in those days consisted of the opinions of a few big zamindars and eminent citizens. Khan Bahadur Hafizullah, Khan Bahadur Imtiaz Hussain, Khalilullah Khan, Khan Bahadur Azizuddin Ahmad of Sherpore, Rai Bahadur Kr. Milap Singh of Madho Tanda, Rai Saheb Bhagwati Prasad, Rai Bahadur Ram Bahadur and Rai Bahadur Shyam Sunder Sahi Saxena and B. Dori Lal and Raja Saheb of Pilibhit constituted the main mouthpiece of the public. With their control and cooperation, the administration could be carried on smoothly. Of these, Rai Bahadur Kr. Milap Singh and Azizuddin Ahmad Khan were shikaris, and their titles were also due to their assistance to the English and other officers in shikar. Pilibhit had dense forests where shikar could be had in plenty.

The public opinion from the grassroots, namely the villages, had not yet developed. Except for B. Mukund Lal and one or two more respectable men of middle classes and intelligentsia, the Congress workers were disgruntled men from families who had nothing at stake, and who were a liability in their families. The Congress was respected because of its goal of independence and because of Gandhiji, Jawaharlal Nehru, Subhash Chandra Bose and other respectable leaders of eminence in whom the masses had faith and for whom a deep respect was growing every day. Their sacrifices and incarcerations affected people deeply. The middle and higher classes mostly kept aloof, lending only their general approbation to the cause and movement. The top levels of the Congress were men of stature and undoubted integrity who had made personal sacrifices, who had given away all their property and family life, and before them the masses and the classes bowed their heads. It was mainly because of them that the movement was growing those days in depth, intensity and in range.

On 24 August 1942, I left by train for Gorakhpur via Lucknow. We were three now. My son Arvind, born in Pilibhit, was not a year and half. I had a fourth person, Dayanidhi Sharma, in the compartment, who boarded at Pooranpur where I had hidden him from my warrant of arrest. It was cloudy, with pools of water shining amidst vast stretches of paddy fields as the train rushed along. The panorama stretched beyond the horizon, and as I gazed upon it, I reflected on the faces left behind at Pilibhit, and looked apprehensively on what was to come at Gorakhpur which was reported to be one of the most disturbed areas of the 1942 movement.

I stayed in Lucknow till 30 August, where my wife and her sister engaged themselves in distributing objectionable Congress literature. My wife's sister was Sita, a student of Mahila Vidyapith College. She was arrested in a demonstration and later released in the evening.

Before I take leave of Pilibhit, I must mention the great charms of the district which I thoroughly enjoyed. Nestling below the great Himalayas and bordering Nepal, the district is largely covered with deep and dense forests. The great Sharda Canal emerges from the Sharda river and passes through the thick jungles of Nainital, Pilibhit and Lakhimpur districts. As Excise Commissioner, UP, I had an occasion to see the source of this great canal, which flows like a big river, forest-fringed on both sides, with big game abounding in the dense growth.

The mighty Sharda river is chained at the headworks near Banbasa, and the temple of Goddess Durga from across Nepal looks down upon the foaming and gurgling waters below. The Canal Inspection House is a beautiful place. As you travel by car along the side of the Sharda Canal, there are tall trees on each side and serene and eerie silence reigns. I have travelled deeper into the forest up to the impenetrable jungles along the Ghaghra river to a village called Dhakka Chat. Here alligators could be found lying in the sunshine along the bank of the river. Pilibhit town on the southern side was a predominantly forest area, with jungles commencing from a distance of about 8 km from the town. I also recall how I, along with my wife and a few-months-old son, had gone on an elephant with a shikar party into the tall grasses in the forests. A night out in these jungles is an experience, when the stars in the sky are the only light, and when the deep silence is broken by the rustle of leaves or sounds of wild animals warning others of a predator or of the intrusion of man.

6

I arrived at Gorakhpur on the morning of 31 August 1942, and called on the Collector. I was immediately given orders to proceed to Bhatni Junction railway station as Special Magistrate, where Brigadier Moore was stationed in command of a large contingent of troops, and shootings were going on. The only instructions by Mr Moss, the Collector, was to control the Brigadier who was shooting people at random, and also to restore normal civil conditions. I was also warned from annoying the Brigadier as he had been an ADC to the Viceroy.

Gorakhpur was the biggest district of UP. Deoria district, that was constituted in 1949, was still a part of it. There were thus eight tehsils and SDOs. There was an ADM, K.B. Usman Ali Khan at Gorakhpur, and another ADM I.U. Alexander at Deoria. Gorakhpur was a Muslim-dominated city, under the complete control of the Muslim League, which had dissociated itself from the national movement.

Mian Saheb was the religious leader with an English wife. The president of the UP Muslim League was a big zamindar of Gorakhpur. The Hindu officers were suspects, and the Muslim officers led by Khan Saheb Zaheer Alam Ansari, Deputy Collector (who later migrated to Pakistan) were not very friendly to Hindu officers. The district also consisted of big rajas like the Raja of Tamkuhi, and the Raja of Majholi. The Mahant of Gorakhpur, Digvijay Nath, was a staunch Hindu of the Hindu Mahasabha and a suspect for the Englishmen and also an eyesore for the Muslim League.

However, Habib Ahmad Siddiqui, SDO Sadar, was as good a man as can be. Ansari was reported to be having the ear of Collector Moss. He, and later two Hindu officers, had been sent as liaison officers and Special Magistrates to assist Brigadier Moore. But they had failed and had been recalled.

Gorakhpur was also full of Englishmen. Most of the sugar factories had Englishmen as general managers. The notorious Willoughby, formerly an indigo cultivating zamindar, was a big zamindar in the Tamkuhi area, and a harsh and cruel master to his large peasantry. There were other landowning English planters. The Collector, the SP, and the DIG, all being Englishmen, were friendly with them. The White Club was the preserve of the white men, and even the Indian ICS Commissioner Wajahat Hussein was not its member. For the Indians, there was the Nepal Club.

Moss was famous for having tried and sentenced Pandit Jawaharlal Nehru to four years in prison in 1940. In 1942, the Civil Disobedience movement had broken out in processions and demonstrations which were crushed by firings and killings. Gorakphur had a large border with Bihar in the east. This side of Bihar was in great turmoil. Wild rumours were afloat as correct news was not available since the press was gagged under the Defence of India rules. Many railway stations from Bhatni to Banaras had been burnt down, and railway services were completely disrupted. Only one train operated between Gorakhpur and Chhapra in the daytime. Fishplates from the tracks had been removed and railway and telegraph poles had been pulled down. People listened to secret radio networks. I, too, had listened to some banned broadcasts giving information on how to commit acts of sabotage.

Fines were imposed and recovered mercilessly whenever acts of sabotage were reported, and firings and shootings of innocent men were the order of the day. The general public in the villages were quaking with apprehension and fear. That was the state of affairs when I arrived at Bhatni around 11 a.m. on 1 September 1942, accompanied by an orderly peon and my Peshkar. I reflected on my unenviable situation. My goods were in transit, I had no home, my wife and child were in Lucknow, and I, at just twenty-eight years of age, was a stranger amongst inhospitable men.

The station was full of army men. I put myself up in the first-class waiting room, stuck a nameplate of 'Special Magistrate' and asked for some food to be arranged. I then sat in an armchair assessing the situation.

At 4 p.m., Brigadier Moore came to my room and asked me whether I was the magistrate posted at Bhatni. When I said yes, we shook hands. He then told me that his prisoners were eating away all his rations and they had to be disposed of. As he was going out in a patrol train somewhere, he directed his Subedar to attend to me and the prisoners. I found that on one side in a yard, two or three train compartments had been kept and they were full of prisoners arrested by the army. I made enquiries from each of them and classified them as follows:

1. Those who were Congress leaders arrested for being in the movement.
2. Those who had participated in some procession or demonstration.
3. Those who had committed acts of sabotage.
4. Ordinary thieves or bad characters arrested at the instance of the police.
5. Innocent men just rounded up to create terror.

I disposed them off like this:

1. I made warrants of detention for the first category and directed that they be sent to Gorakhpur next morning.

2. The second and third category I tried in court and sentenced them to various terms of imprisonment.
3. The fourth category of persons were sent to Deoria for trial.
4. The last category, which consisted of 50 per cent of the prisoners, I disposed of more summarily. I put on my most threatening manner, asked them to fall in a line, hold their ears, sit and stand up ten times, and then run home as fast as their legs could carry.

The Brigadier arrived that night, and finding the bogey of prisoners empty, the next morning came up to me and asked me how I had done this. I explained to him my classification and told him that I had given the first category of Congress rebels indefinite terms of imprisonment, the second and third category seven years, the fourth was the domain of police administration, and that I had frightened the fifth category out of their wits and that they would all behave. He was mighty pleased, shook my hand, and told me that I was the magistrate after his heart.

I had by next day gauged the situation. One had to wear a fearful look and appear unbendingly harsh in outlook to gain the Brigadier's confidence and to have control of the situation. When the train with the prisoners who had been tried and sentenced left, they shouted 'Mahatma Gandhi Ki Jai'. The General Manager of the sugar factory in Bhatni immediately informed the Brigadier, who asked me if they had shouted such a slogan. I assumed an even more excited manner and angrily asked the manager why he did not inform me at once. Then I shouted at the station master and told him to call the train back so that I could have all of them shot. I told the Brigadier that I had given them seven years and their back would be broken ultimately, so he agreed to drop the matter. It was necessary under the circumstances to gain his confidence to be able to do any administrative good at the time.

I was able to gather some more information after some time. On 31 August 1942, Brigadier Moore and the English medical officer of the army, with a few army jawans, had gone to a village named Deoghat some kilometres from Bhatni. The zamindar of the village had a big pucca brick house. An elephant was tied in front of his house indicating his high status. Now the Brigadier summoned the zamindar and asked him to pay a collective fine of Rs 2000 immediately, as he would have certainly committed some act of treason. The zamindar trembled and begged for mercy, but the Brigadier, after a few minutes doubled the fine, and asked him to pay this amount, or he would treble the amount. The poor man went into his huge house and bolted from the back door and ran away to Motihari in Bihar. In the meanwhile, the Brigadier waited and then fired two rounds with his revolver. At this, the elephant took fright and became restive. Then two men who used to handle the elephant came with their spears to control the elephant, but the Brigadier, thinking they were coming to attack him, shot them dead. He then went back, got more men, pillaged the whole house, carried away all the gold jewellery found on the women, as well as ninety bags of wheat which he deposited in the army store room.

On my third day here, the Brigadier himself narrated the story to me. He was sorry he had killed the men who were trying to control the elephant, but the zamindar had to pay the fine. If that scoundrel Misra did not pay the fine of Rs 4000, he said, he would feel the greatest pleasure in pulling down his pucca house. To this I added my own threats that if Zamindar Misra did not turn up and pay the fine, I would spread kerosene oil on his crops and burn them. This pleased the Brigadier and he said that now he would leave the matter entirely in my hands. Immediately I added that he come to the village with me and pay Rs 500 to each of the two widows out of the fines collected already. He agreed and this was done the same evening.

The next day, I told my men to contact Misra and tell him that I had asked him to come meet me with the Rs 4000 fine. I promised him that in good time the amount would be returned, and I guaranteed his security. After three days, Misra turned up in the evening. He put Rs 3000 before me and said he had not been able to arrange the remaining one thousand but that he would deposit it the next day. I sent off a note to the Brigadier that his man was in my room. He arrived with two army jawans. I handed over the money to the Brigadier, and explained that Misra would pay the balance the next day. In his broken Hindustani, the Brigadier told Misra that he had behaved like a coward, and that on his account two brave men had lost their lives. He then asked the two jawans to take him to the army-improvised prison. As he was being marched off, Misra threw a most piteous look at me. I indicated that he should not resist but obey the orders. Once he was out of sight, I told the Brigadier that I had promised he would be safe. On hearing this, the Brigadier called his men and asked them to release Misra as desired by the Magistrate.

The next day, the zamindar brought the remaining Rs 1000. I had all his jewellery and the ninety bags of wheat released to him. Later, when the Brigadier left Bhatni, I spoke to Mr Moss over the phone and told him the whole story, and with his permission returned the fine amount of Rs 4000 to Misra. A few years later, I learnt that when Brigadier Moore was leaving Bhatni, Misra, without my knowledge, gave a gold necklace for the Brigadier's wife. This was done on Brigadier Moore's asking.

Once I built up a rapport with the Brigadier, and he was sure I would not do anything prejudicial to His Majesty's Government, and that my attitudes were more or less in conformity with his own, I studied him closely. He was a man six feet tall and a teetotaller. He got up early in the morning and after his small breakfast was ready for work. He had a tremendous amount of energy. He would take his English doctor and a compartment load of armed army men, and in the patrol train he would saunter forth in one or the other direction. They would get down at some place and walk a mile or so into some village and do some pillaging which they called realization of collective fine. They had also been to the trading centre of Barhaj on the Ghaghra river and had ransacked several houses and collected huge sums of money. All the bundles of notes so collected used to be thrust into a large wooden box. This had been the normal routine of Brigadier Moore ever since he and his troops had been posted there after the outbreak of disorder on 10 August 1942.

I came to the conclusion that the only way to control his atrocious activities was first to gain his confidence and then to channel his energies. The entire revenue administration machinery and the police had been suspended in the area. I called up the Tehsildar and Kanungos and asked them to prepare a list of zamindars or big businessmen and collect Rs 25 from each. A list of about fifty persons was prepared. In consultation with them, a programme was drawn up. I decided that the Brigadier and his two officers and I would have lunch and dinner at the Railway Dining Room each day, but every day at 11 a.m. and 4 p.m. a function would be organized at a village at a distance of about one hour's journey on foot. Every zamindar was informed of this date-wise. Then I went to the Brigadier and told him that about a hundred big people and zamindars had come to invite him and his party for lunch and dinner in recognition of his meritorious work in restoring peace. The Brigadier beamed with immense satisfaction. I said I had accepted it on his behalf, but that the lunch and dinner at their cost would be at the station, and for the functions and tea twice a day, we would be going out every day. This worked. Every morning we would go out and walk a mile with the army men. In the village they would be received, and everybody was garlanded. Then tea, cake, dry and fresh fruits would be served and also a speech would be delivered. This completely changed the attitude of these Englishmen, who thought that they were being loved and honoured. At 3 p.m., the same would be repeated. By the time they returned, it would be lunch time or dinner time and so there would hardly be any time for mischief.

Having channelized their energies, I told the Brigadier that now it was high time that normal administrative agencies functioned, namely the police for crime and the revenue agency for realization of land revenue and collective fines. I impressed upon him that these agencies were having a holiday at the expense of the army. This he agreed to, and so I passed orders with a copy to him that no collective fine would be collected by the army and the administrative agencies might function. Thus the opportunity to make mischief was taken away. In the meanwhile, railway tracks had been repaired, the train from Banaras made its first appearance, and I directed that henceforth passengers could come to the stations, which had been prohibited by the army earlier.

One of the invitations made to the Brigadier and his men was from the Raja of Majholi. We went on a horse-drawn ekka, for some distance. Then we crossed the river Choti Gandak in the afternoon. I recall the placid waters and the lazily plying small boat, the half-clad boatmen and the river meandering along the maize fields. When we reached the palace of the Raja of Majholi, we were taken to his big durbar-like drawing room where a large number of easy chairs were laid. One by one, more than half-a-dozen sons of the raja came and seated themselves, and this went on for over twenty minutes. Then came the raja, a man of about sixty. Tea was served. In the course of his conversation, he told Brigadier Moore that all the disturbances in that area were due to one man and that this person was not allowing the raja to construct an important road as it would pass through his field. The Brigadier turned to me and asked whether the construction of a road was a good thing or not. When I said that it would be good if a road came up, he observed that a person who did not allow the construction of a road must be a bad man, and should be punished. I assured him that I would punish the man and send him to jail.

By this time I had shifted to the Railway Rest House at the back of the station. The next day, the Brigadier asked me what I had done about the bad man. I told him that I had asked the Station House Officer (SHO) of the police station concerned to send him to me. I had actually done no such thing and had counted on his forgetting the matter. The next day he again came to me and said that as the SHO was delaying this, I should give a letter to him for the SHO, and he would send a patrol train to fetch the man. I wrote out a note, and a patrol train was sent to fetch him. The man was brought and lodged in the army lock-up.

The next day, around 11 a.m., the ASP of the Deoria sub-division came to me and protested the arrest of the man. He said that this man and the Raja of Majholi had a dispute about this piece of land since 1857, and that the matter had gone up to the Privy Council in London and the field had been declared to belong to this man. The raja had used our visit as an opportunity to dispossess and harass the man who had stood loyal to the British. I asked him to go and speak to the Brigadier. But the ASP said he couldn't, as he was Irish and the English Brigadier did not trust him. So I wrote a note to the Brigadier on the above lines, and mentioned that as Magistrate of the area, I would order the man's release. The Brigadier came to meet me, but since I was sleeping then, left a note saying he was sending the man back in a patrol train.

Another incident was fraught with more serious consequences. The train from Gorakhpur had arrived around 11 a.m., and there was a crowd at the station. I was there and was talking to a Patwari about his realization of collective fines. He told me that all the villages except one had paid. Just then the Brigadier passed by, overheard it, and asked who would not pay. Before I could intervene, the Patwari named the village. In order to prevent the Brigadier and his men going to the village where they might resort to shooting and burning, I told the Patwari to meet us at the railway track near the village, along with all the villagers. The village was beyond Bankata railway station towards Siwan in Chhapra district of Bihar, about 1.5 km in the interior.

The patrol train was commandeered, a bogey of armed army men was taken, and we left for the destination. I suggested that we would go on to Siwan and stop at the village on our return. I did this to gain some more time and for the villagers to gather at the spot. The Brigadier agreed and I told the Patwari to make sure that the villagers came there within one hour. To my dismay, on our return after an hour, I found that not more than four people had gathered. The Brigadier and the whole platoon of about a hundred armed soldiers got down and started marching to the village. It was cloudy and fields stretched on both sides, pools of water shone lending lustre to the gold and green of the paddy leaves and plants. There was peace and stillness in the afternoon air. I reflected on what was to come—shooting and burning of a village before my eyes, all my attempts to save the area from rampage and devastation having come to naught. The faces of my wife Parvati and sister-in-law Sita flashed in my mind's eye—their eyes held only contempt and rebuke for me.

We reached a large mango grove near the small village. The jawans fell into a formation for action, and the Brigadier announced that if in five minutes the villagers did not turn up, it would give him the greatest pleasure to burn the village down. He stood with a time piece in his hand. I stood and watched in consternation. Just then, an idea occurred to me and I can only believe that it was God who came to my rescue. I thought that if I went out into the village, Brigadier Moore would not burn it till I came out. So I told him that I suspected some foul play was up, and would like to go into the village to investigate. Then accompanied by two jawans whom he sent with me, I went in.

In the village, I found men going about lazily, some drawing water from the well. The Patwari, the headman, the chowkidar and I ordered them to come out and proceed to the grove. In the process I beat up with my cane some lazy men who did not know that calamity was hovering about their heads. By the time I emerged from the village, about fifty villagers had collected in the grove. A few had brought some money, the majority had not. However, I did not allow the initiative to pass from my hand. I pretended to check some papers that I took out from my pocket, then walked up to the Brigadier, pretending to be in a great temper. Then I told him that I had found out that the Patwari was a non-resident one (I explained to him what a resident and non-resident Patwari meant) and that he had never been here. He only wanted us to collect the collective fine for him, and that most of the villagers had already paid. To make this all the more convincing, I threatened the Patwari with my cane. I told him that he must collect the Rs 284 collective fine due and deposit it the next day at Bhatni or he would be in the lock-up. The Brigadier joined in and called the Patwari a scoundrel, but stood down his men. We all marched back to our waiting patrol train.

The evening had fallen, and in the midst of a silvery cloud with a streak of gold lining, the sun was going down below the tops of the tall trees. I felt beholden to my Maker, who stood by me and helped me prevent a great disaster. As I lay in bed that night, I felt the gentle smiling eyes of my wife looking at me, serene and full of affection and pride.

Having established a friendly rapport with the Brigadier, I now suggested to him that having wielded a strong stick in the area, and having restored law and order, it was necessary now to build up the morale of the people and reward the good men who had been loyal and had helped us. He agreed most readily. The Naib Tehsildar drew up a list of all the men from whom collective fine had been realized indicating the amount. I took the list to Brigadier Moore who approved it as the list of good men. All of them were called up one day and lined up. Bundles of notes were taken out from the wooden box and placed in a large basket carried by an army Subedar. I read out each name, indicating the amount of reward, and the Brigadier gave it out. There was only one case where he refused to hand out the money. It was to one Sundar Tiwari. With a queer and fantastic observation, he said, 'Brahmins are the lowest of the low, and Tiwaris are the worst.' And so he would not give the reward to this Tiwari.

Another incident occurred when the Brigadier decided to loot and pillage Hatwa Bazar, which was about 1.5 km from Bhatni station. He came to me one morning and told me that he had a fine proposal. He argued that Hatwa Bazar was a big bazaar inhabited by many well-to-do persons, and if the army had not been stationed at Bhatni, they would certainly have participated in the rebellious disturbances, and so a collective fine should be realized from them! I was taken aback at this logic and concluded that after keeping his violent tendencies in check for some time, he now had an urge to go back to his old ways. By this time, I was more in command of the general situation. So I told the Brigadier that it was also likely that they would not have rebelled. He realized the possibility and went back to his apartment.

The next day he came again and urged that his information was that they would have certainly rebelled at Hatwa Bazar. By now I was fed up, and put my foot down. I told him that nobody at Hatwa had been about to break the law and I would simply not allow any action. The Brigadier went away. He came back the next day with another proposal. He told me that Hatwa Bazar consisted of many money-lending Baniyas, and money-lenders were bad men. So in order to punish the bad men, and build up the morale of the peasantry in debt, we should go, raid their premises, seize the account books, burn them all, and inform the villagers that their debts have been wiped out.

I told the Brigadier that the main hurdle here was that there were good money-lenders as well as bad money-lenders or extortionists, and it was hard to distinguish between the two. But that was still not the end of it. He returned the next day saying he had prepared a list of bad money-lenders, and gave the list to me. He suggested that we might go and raid the houses of just these people. I took the list to examine it. Then I called the SHO of the GRP

(Police), and asked him to throw some light as to who was advising the Brigadier. He gave me the name of a dismissed police head constable. The man had been dismissed for graft and misconduct, and was now an adviser to Moore.

Armed with this information I wrote a note to the Brigadier objecting to the list, and also bringing to his notice that according to my information he was being advised by a man who was a dismissed head constable and a very undesirable person. The Brigadier summoned the man, threatened him, and dismissed him. Thus ended this episode.

Brigadier Moore left Bhatni with his contingent on 15 September 1942 on transfer to Lucknow, but not before he had spoken to Mr Moss about what he termed as my sterling qualities.

Brigadier Moore was replaced by another English Major whose troops were entirely British. He did not interfere in my work and his instructions appeared to be to assist me and to be handy and available.

By this time, I had shifted to the railway bungalow about a furlong from the railway station, and I breathed easy. It was an old, tiled, big bungalow type house with a veranda and two rooms. There was a maize field in the back, and paddy fields on two sides. There were mango groves close by, and a big neem tree in which we put up a rope jhoola (swing). My wife had arrived from Lucknow with my one year and ten months old son. We hardly had any personal effects except some necessary clothes and a few kitchen utensils. Food stocks were purchased week to week. So we lived unfettered by worldly possessions which close upon ones growing life like a prison house, and prevent its flowering. Both of us were in our youth with a sunlit life ahead. We would go out some evenings on our patrol train to scenic spots. I recall an evening when we halted our train along a lazily flowing river with a solitary boatman plying his boat. As evening fell, the golden hues of the sky were reflected in the waters. We watched silently till, under the darkening horizon, the figure of the boat and the boatman got blurred and disappeared into the darkness. In this house we found peace and happiness, and felt the tranquility of the still air, the blue sky, the music of the birds and the murmuring rustle of maize leaves all around.

Thus we lived, making a daily patrol of one railway line or the other, till one day we got a jolt. On the night of 25-26 September, at about 3 a.m., I received a telegram from the station master of Bhanta Pokhar railway station, 14 km on this side of Siwan in Bihar province. It said that the fishplates had been removed, poles uprooted, and the track damaged. It was clearly a Bihar government matter. Mr Moss had, however, instructed me that the Governor General had asked him to be responsible for this part of Bihar also. Since this would also affect the running of trains to Gorakhpur, I got the station master to ask the Engineering and Repairing unit to get ready. I also alerted the commander of the British force. I took all in the patrol train and reached the spot around 6.30 a.m. The villagers had collected, and said they gave chase to the saboteur. The engineering unit went into action, the poles were again put up, and I got the villagers to trace out the shoes and some instruments used by the saboteurs. By the time we did all of this, the patrol train reached from Siwan with the SDM of Siwan. I handed over the confiscated articles to him and left for Bhatni. I sent a full report to Mr Moss who, I understand, sent it on to prove his superiority to the Bihar government.

I would like to mention here some heroic aspects of the national movement. In the first week of September 1942, when I was installed at the railway station, I expressed a desire to one of my old class fellows to meet my old teacher Pandit Naresh Prasad Misra. I had been a student of the Government High School, Deoria, in the years 1926-30. I had been a distinguished student and was remembered there as I had stood 1st class 1st in UP from the school. Pandit Naresh Prasad Misra was my most respected teacher who had been an inspiration for me. Panditji lived in a village not far from Bhatni.

On the news being conveyed to him that the Special Magistrate wanted to meet him, he came himself and was announced to me. When I touched his feet, he was overwhelmed. He told me that he had come with some money as collective fine. He then told me with tears in his eyes that his only son, Saryu Prasad Misra, a staunch Congressman and a leading figure in the movement, had been arrested and was lodged in Deoria jail. His daughter-in-law was completely distraught with grief, and Panditji himself was unable to bear the separation and grief. He broke into tears. I said I would release his son. After a few days when my credit was fully established with Collector Moss, I told him the whole story and my interest in the matter. Moss authorized me to release Saryu Prasad Misra. When I informed Pandit Naresh Prasad that the Collector had agreed to release his son, he told me not to go ahead. Saryu Prasad was a man of principles and was a devoted Congressman, true to Gandhiji and the country. He wanted to go through the suffering of incarceration and imprisonment like the rest of the patriots in the country. If he came to know that he had been released because his father and wife could not endure the suffering, he would be most unhappy. He did not want to be responsible for destroying his son's idealism. Pandit Naresh Prasad told me that I, too, was like a son to him, and I should not destroy his son by releasing him. So I did not.

There were many such instances of heroism and idealism inspired by Gandhiji's self-sacrificing movement.

I cannot forget that day in Gorakhpur when Shibban Lal Saxena, the veteran Congress leader of Maharajganj tehsil, was arrested and great was the glee in British circles about this. Nor can I forget the face of Shibban Lal Saxena when I visited the jail along with the Collector J.L.C. Stubbs, and found him standing in a cell meant for condemned prisoners, erect and undaunted, his ankles and wrists in iron fetters. That was the spirit generated by Gandhiji—the greatness of the human spirit over the body, and outside forces were made mundane.

On 16 October 1942, I left Bhatni for Gorakhpur having finished my task. The District Magistrate felt that no further precautions were necessary as normalcy had returned everywhere. I was seen off at the railway station by a large crowd who at that time felt I had remained there as a saviour in those troubled times. In any case I had the satisfaction of my conscience, and at the same time I stood high in the estimation of my British masters.

I remained in Gorakhpur from 1942 to 1946. I should say a word here about the Quit India Movement as it operated in Pilibhit and Gorakhpur. It was called 'Congress Rebellion' at the time and stood completely contained by 31 August 1942, in less than three weeks. The major leaders had been arrested, the processions lathi-charged or fired upon, the saboteurs sent to jail with sentences of long imprisonment, and the administration took repressive measures at the least provocation. Some atrocities got perpetrated in the process which struck terror, and the general masses stood aloof plying their business or plough as usual. The control of essential commodities under the Defence of India Rules threw the business community completely at the mercy of administration. A new class of agents, or permit holders and licensees, sprang up who were the henchmen of the administration and threatened to usurp the regular traders. In this way the administration was in complete command of all the trade and business.

Rent control measures, petrol rationing and control of grain markets, cloth and kerosene further tightened the noose around the public. Even when Gandhiji's death was deemed imminent on account of his twenty-one-day fast in 1943, and the orders were given that no demonstration or hartal be countenanced, my assessment at that time in Gorakhpur was that merely ripples would have occurred, should that event have come about. Every Indian must have suffered intensely, the conscience of many would have revolted. Some officers might have resigned as R.N. Dey, ICS, did. But by and large, nothing would have happened to disturb the even tenor of public life. The Indian public, at least in Gorakhpur, lay still and helpless at the feet of their master, who with steely attitude fought the Germans with their back to the wall.

I dare say, on the basis of what I saw and felt at the time, that the Quit India Movement lay soon in shambles, and the British, if they so wished, could have continued to rule without much trouble. It was more their weak economic and political position after the Second World War that forced them to grant Independence. It must, however, be mentioned that though the public lay speechless and helpless, the hatred of the British entered every heart and soul. The overbearing attitude of the British masters was galling, and all self-respecting Indians felt humiliated. Gandhiji's continued imprisonment, Kasturba's death in jail, his fast, the detention of great leaders like Pandit Jawaharlal Nehru, Maulana Azad and a host of others hurt and pained every Indian. Many felt that they were committing a sin by tolerating the alien rule. Meanwhile, the broadcasts of Subhash Chandra Bose kept up the spirit, and held out hopes of an ultimate Independence. Every victory of the British was received coldly, and every advance of the Germans was hailed privately. And when the Japanese advanced like a speedy avalanche, the Indians felt happy and many looked upon them as liberators. It is indeed a miracle of history that so much hatred of the British was turned into goodwill and cooperation by Lord Mountbatten later.

Gorakhpur had three District Magistrates in my time, namely Mr Moss, Mr I.U. Alexander for a few months, and Mr J.L.C. Stubbs. Stubbs succeeded Moss when the latter left for Lucknow as War Production Commissioner. I was Town Control Magistrate for a few months and then District Supply Officer. I recall a few incidents from this time.

In 1943, as a grain control measure, orders were issued under Section 81 of the Defence of India rules, that every person had to declare within a specified period the grain stocks held by them if it exceeded five maunds. Amongst the several returns received, one was from a Khan Bahadur who at that time was officiating as President of the Muslim League in UP. As the return was received very much after the prescribed time, the usual notice was issued to him to explain why the return was submitted late and why action should not be taken. Khan Bahadur Saheb wrote an impertinent letter to me taking exception to this, and mentioning that as an important person, the notice should not have been issued to him. The matter was taken up by Khan Saheb Zahir Alam Ansari and ADM K.B. Usman Ali Khan, who supported his stand and told me that I should apologize, for which I saw absolutely no reason. They whipped up a campaign against me and wrote to Collector Moss to take me to task. When Moss arrived from Lucknow to hand over charge to J.L.C. Stubbs—it was the official custom and tradition those days that the outgoing District Magistrate settled all outstanding issues and gave his opinions on various problems to his successor, to maintain continuity—Khan Saheb Ansari and Usman Ali went and saw Mr Moss about this pending issue. They told him that I should apologize. I did not know what transpired. Moss left at night for Lucknow and J.L.C. Stubbs was the Collector next day.

I was preparing to call on Stubbs, when at 9 a.m. Khan Bahadur Saheb arrived at my house. He told me that he had come to offer his apologies to me for the impertinent letter he had written, and requested me to drop the matter. I assured him that it was a routine notice, and that the matter be treated as closed. Then I went and called on Stubbs around 10 a.m. The first question that Stubbs asked me was whether the Khan Bahadur had apologized to me or not. On my replying that he had done so, Stubbs mentioned that it had been conveyed to Khan Bahadur last night that unless he apologized to me by 9 a.m. he would be prosecuted and warrants of arrest would be issued.

In another incident, I had tried a case for theft of a sewing machine belonging to a missionary Englishwoman of Chauri Chaura. The case had ended in acquittal. One day, the woman came up in court and accused me of partiality and charged me with dishonesty, saying the person had been acquitted because she had not paid my bribe. I trembled with indignation, but could not do anything to the Englishwoman. I wrote out a note to Stubbs who in turn wrote to her that unless she apologized to me, he would have her arrested and prosecuted. She did turn up and offered profuse apologies.

There were various other instances of the fair-mindedness of the Englishmen and the support they gave to their subordinates. As District Supply Officer, I made allotment of coal wagons to sugar factories. In some monthly allotments, Mairwa Sugar Factory did not receive as much as they had wanted. So the General Manager, an Englishman and a friend of I.U. Alexander, wrote to me an impertinent letter accusing me of dishonest allotment, and threatening to bring my conduct to the notice of the Collector to whom a copy was endorsed. I.U. Alexander, a bachelor, used to visit this Englishman. The manager would also come and stay with Alexander in the Collector's house. I was in the midst of some important meeting when I received his letter and was filled with bitter indignation. I was only thirty then. As I contemplated protesting to the Collector in a note, I received a sealed envelope from him, which contained a letter from I.U. Alexander to the General Manager. In the letter, Alexander expressed his annoyance and displeasure at the tone and content of the letter, and asked him to tender apologies to me on the pain of his entire quota of coal being cut off. I received the letter of apologies soon after. The English District Magistrates always stood by their subordinates and were fair and just in their administrative outlook except of course, where His Majesty's Government was threatened.

I had occasion to watch J.L.C. Stubbs from close quarters. He was neat and tidy in outlook and habits, very fair-minded and exceptionally honest, and maintained integrity even in small details. When petrol rationing was introduced, he took to the bicycle for going to court. He was always for strictness in official work and discipline, and also enjoined integrity in conduct and behaviour. He would stand no nonsense and was always for fair play. He stood behind his officers like a rock and encouraged initiative. Where he thought that my proposals had originality, he wrote to the Secretary Food and Supplies, bringing my talent to his notice and giving all the credit to me. This is quite unlike present bosses who want to take credit for everything actually done by their subordinates.

One incident stands out in my mind. Woollen cloth was controlled, and a permit system had been introduced allotting a quota to each department for the employees. There was only one cloth agent, a businessman of substance. The Kotwal of the city asked him to reserve cloth for the police when the next instalment arrived, and if he did not do so, he would be arrested and prosecuted. The businessman came to me and asked me to release some cloth in his favour so that he could give it to the police. I did not agree and distributed the cloth as usual according to the permit system. This infuriated the Kotwal who handcuffed the agent, paraded him, and took him through the main bazaar to the kotwali. It was evening, and despite telephone calls from me and the Deputy SP L.B. Baijal, they did not release him on bail. Stubbs, who was going to Lucknow, asked me to give him a full report on his return. I made the report and took it to him.

Stubbs called up I.M. Hurrel, SP, and within an hour the Kotwal was suspended. He was chargesheeted and a departmental inquiry commenced. C. Mull, Deputy SP, who was conducting the inquiry, had instructions to submit the report the same day, and the Kotwal was to be summarily dismissed. In order to avoid bad blood between the supply department and police, I requested Mr Hurrel to revoke the suspension orders. He felt Stubbs was in a furious mood and he dared not appear soft and lenient. I met Stubbs with him, and due to my equation with Stubbs, somehow succeeded in getting the suspension order revoked. Stubbs observed that the departmental inquiry would proceed because, to quote him, power had gone to the heads of the underlings after 1942, and it was necessary to discipline them and restore sanity and discipline.

Another incident occurred at Gorakhpur, concerning the Tehsildar of Pharenda. H.S. Bates was Commissioner of Gorakhpur, and had gone to Balrampur where he had been manager of the estate. Pharenda railway station was enroute. The train arrived around midnight. The Tehsildar of Pharenda, Thakur Baijnath Singh, a hefty thakur, came to board the train and knocked on the first-class compartment in which the Commissioner was travelling. He knocked louder and louder with his cane, till the Commissioner was awakened and opened the door. The Tehsildar entered the compartment and took Mr Bates to task for having kept him waiting like this and that it was bad manners. Pharenda tehsil had many Englishmen as zamindars and managers in the sugar factories and he obviously took the Commissioner for one of them. The Commissioner was a suave person, who got him to cool down, and even offered him his cigarettes. Later, as the next station was approaching, the Commissioner asked him his name and credentials and Singh replied in a tone of authority that he was the Tehsildar of Pharenda and asked him who he was. When the Commissioner mentioned his name and that he was Commissioner Gorakhpur Division, the Tehsildar was at a loss on what to do. As soon as the next station came, he made a beeline for the exit and disappeared fast from there. We had all gone to receive the Commissioner at the railway station. However, H.S. Bates went to the exit gate, and on seeing Baijnath Singh slinking away, caught him by the shoulders and requested him to collect his luggage which he had been taking care of all the time. The Commissioner later narrated the entire story, which he said he had thoroughly enjoyed, and directed the Collector to forget it completely.

A word must be mentioned here about the Indians in the ICS. Most of them were distinguished men like V.N. Mehta, Dr Panna Lal, V.P. Sathe, Wajahat Hussain, Hifazat Hussain, Hasan Zaheer, B.N. Jha, Bhagwan Sahai, Vishnu Sahai and Shanker Prasad. They had glorious records under the British, and made themselves felt. But there were others who merely bossed over the Indian subordinates, and made no attempt to improve their learning or competence as so many Englishmen had done, specially in the field of research in ancient Indian customs and history. Administratively and socially, the Englishmen did not admit them into their fold and many of them were disinclined to mingle with other Indians and those in the Provincial Services. Wajahat Hussain, Commissioner Gorakhpur, was a notable exception who even cycled down to my house and the houses of many others. He was a man of culture and made no distinctions. But most of them, disowned by the British, hung in lone splendour.

Before I take leave of Gorakhpur, I would like to mention some aspects of this great region. In my time it was a district where the population was high, and poverty was great. A great many labourers had migrated to Mauritius and the Far East hundreds of years ago. In my own time, the Labour Depot supplying labour to the army was established at Gorakhpur. This was the land trodden by the great Buddha. Lumbini, the place where Lord Buddha was born, lay just across the border of the district. Kasia, or Kushinagar, now in Deoria district, formed part of this district in my time. A little beyond Domakhand jungles into the Nepal territory was a place called Tribeni on the great Narayani river, where a fair or mela was held. It was believed locally that the great Puranic battle in Satya yuga between a tusker elephant and a crocodile took place here, and Lord Shiva intervened when the tusker, whose strength was failing, lifted up his trunk in plaintive supplication.

Across the river, in the mountains, I was shown the place where Sage Valmiki had his hermitage, and where Sita on being abandoned by Rama, stayed and gave birth to the twins Kush and Luv. Gorakhpur is also famous for the Chauri Chaura episode of 1921, which made Gandhiji call a halt to his Satyagraha movement.

An All India Music Conference was organized here in 1944, in aid of War Funds. Acchan Maharaj, the famous Kathak dancer, gave his performance on an improvised stage under a shamiana. There was a large gathering, and Acchan Maharaj's dance was the last item, kept purposely so, in order to keep up the interest of the audience. Dressed in red with kajal smeared on his eyes, the almost sixty-year-old stalwart of Kathak appeared on the stage. Seeing him, some younger members of the audience burst into mocking laughter and nearly hooted him off the stage. At this time, Maheshwar Dayal, a great patron of music and posted at that time as District Judge of Basti, made a small speech and begged the audience to give Acchan Maharaj an opportunity to perform. When finally Acchan Maharaj gave his superb performance, the whole gathering was spellbound, and there was pindrop silence. In the end there was a frantic applause. He had performed for two full hours. The expressions on his face, the ease with which he moved gracefully like a swan on that rough stage was a sight to see. Even today I can recall how he showed the expressions of Krishna and Radha on his face. A loving frown on Radha's face, and an expression of mischief on Krishna's. There was also a mesmerizing jugalbandi between Acchan Maharaj as he danced with wonderful footwork, and Anokhey Lal, the famous tabla player.

Before I take leave of the British days and the British Raj, I must give my assessment of the contribution and performance of the Englishmen as Collectors and administrators. By and large they were a devoted band of officers who wanted to be fair and ensure that no injustice was done to poor people in the villages, and also see that scales of justice were evenly held between several sections of the community. They worked hard, and there was no question of bypassing situations and problems.

In my training as a Junior Officer, both G.W.M. Whittle and J.K. Coghill took a keen interest, going through my diaries and reports. They took me out on tours and explained how things were to be done. Never did any of the English Collectors ask me to go out of my way to do things that were not straight. In Hardoi, my Peshkar advised me on 30 September 1936 to come to court early at 9.30 a.m., to have all the pending revenue cases called out, and dismiss them all as being in default so that on 1 October, I could show a nil pending statement. In my weekly meetings with G.W.M. Whittle I related this, whereupon he asked me whether it was correct and straightforward. He directed me never to do it again and never to do anything that was improper.

The Englishmen were accustomed to the rule of law in their own country, and saw to it that the rule of law was enforced in India, even against the highest. Thus the masses had complete faith in the fair mindedness of the English administrators.

The English administrators trusted their officers. The District Officer was the kingpin in the administrative system, even as he is today, and that officer was judiciously selected by the Governor. Complete confidence was reposed in him. He in turn trusted his officers and gave them complete protection, though there was no question of his protecting or suffering an incompetent or a dishonest officer. When Lord Cornwallis built up the civil service, he laid down three cardinal principles:

1. Recruit them young and train them
2. Trust them
3. Pay them well

This system was strictly adhered to by the British government till 1946. Today all these three pillars of civil service have been almost razed to the ground. The age of recruitment has been raised from twenty-five to twenty-eight. Though training schools have been established, they are academic. The District Officers have no time or inclination to train. There are emergency recruitments where men above thirty-five and forty are selected and a heterogenous, individualistic cadre of incongruous tendencies is created. So far as trusting them is concerned, they are not only not trusted but are vulnerable to the machinations of local politicians. They are an underpaid lot who cannot make both ends meet and are expected to keep their head above water, while their families and finances are sinking fast.

Another quality which characterized these Englishmen was their keenness and anxiety to know the people, the peasantry, their customs and traditions and how life ran in the villages. They rode on horseback and went into the interiors. In winter camps they took interest in redressing grievances, in having first-hand knowledge of the people and their problems. They also kept a check on the conduct and performance of their own Field Officers.

The great pains with which the Englishmen went about their work was witnessed by me when R.M. Marshsmith organized the Air Raid Precautions organization that later became Town Rationing Organization. He looked into each detail. The English revenue settlement officers engaged in land records and settlement work went from field to field and village to village, making classifications of soils, writing out land record details and making valuations of land on the basis of principles prevalent or handed down from the time of Mughals or even earlier systems.

These civil servants dug up archaeological items lost to us. Mr Shirreff who was Commissioner, Faizabad, and later Member, Board of Revenue, was engaged on a research project on Jayasi, the Muslim Sufi poet who wrote *Padmavat* in Hindi. He called me twice, having known my interest in Hindi to discuss with me some aspects of Jayasi. These English civilians came imbued with a sense of values and many of them were a band of scholars. By and large they were all men of integrity, upright and of unblemished public character.

7

I left Gorakhpur in January 1946, and the interim government was formed in March 1946 at the Centre and in the states. I was in Kanpur on 15 August 1947, and went to Lucknow to see the Indian flag being hoisted amidst great enthusiasm. The crowds went berserk with joy. I recalled Gokhale saying that happy were they who could visualize an independent India, happier they who worked for it, but happiest they who lived to see it. I heard the melodious and ringing broadcast of the poet and Governor of UP Sarojini Naidu. And we were in for a new era.

Here I would like to mention the elections held in February 1946. I was Presiding Officer at Kanpur at a polling station near the Parade Ground for the Muslim seat. A nationalist Muslim was pitted against the Muslim League candidate. The supporters of the nationalist candidate were in a hopeless minority in the compound of the school building, which was the polling station. The Muslim

League voters crowded the whole compound menacingly, and the onrush of voters was almost unmanageable. The goonda leaders of the city were authorized agents of the Muslim League candidate. The young enthusiastic boys of Aligarh Muslim University were there to marshal the voters. I needed all my tact and resourcefulness to commandeer these boys and these agents into constructive cooperation in the management of voting. Their hold was complete on the surging crowds who almost to a man voted Muslim League.

Meanwhile the communal disturbances and riots had started in July-August 1947 in the wake of the decision on the formation of Pakistan. The upsurge of communal passions was tremendous, and all traditional ties and neighbourly feelings were swept away in a wave of hatred and violence. I was transferred to Saharanpur and placed in charge of the UP and East Punjab boundary where killings and the uprooting of Muslims and the surging waves of incoming refugees were the main problems. Much has been written since on the carnage and the great upheaval. I don't want to talk much on this, but will mention a few incidents which may be of interest.

The river Yamuna formed the boundary of Saharanpur and East Punjab on the west. When the Muslims in the villages across were being killed or hounded out by the vengeful refugees coming from West Pakistan, a young Muslim married girl, hardly eighteen years of age, sought refuge in the jungles across the river. A young Gujjar of the nearby village in Saharanpur district came across her, took her home, married her and she stayed as his wife. This was in August-September 1947. Late in 1948, Mridula Sarabhai started her movement for recovery and restoration of women left behind in India and Pakistan. This woman was on the list. Her husband came from Pakistan, found out her whereabouts, and applied to me for her production in court. She was recovered under a search warrant and produced before me. She stood in court with her two husbands on either side and a small baby about three months old in her arms. She had a pleasant and soft face and big eyes. I asked her to relate her story and she narrated the incidents as given above. I then put it to her whether she wanted to go with her former husband, or stay with her current Gujjar husband. I recall vividly how her big moist eyes looked at one and then at the other helplessly. Then she observed that though her Gujjar husband had given her all the love and affection, she would like to go with her former Muslim husband. The Gujjar man started weeping and requested her to let him have the baby as a reminder of her. She kept clinging to the child, but finally handed him over to the weeping father. It was a pathetic sight. How many women suffered similarly and how many of these suffering women had their emotional ties uprooted time and again. We can only try to understand the extent of misery and suffering of all such women.

The refugees from Pakistan had their own share of struggles. There were many making a new life in Saharanpur. With everything in ruins and all that they loved left behind, these indomitable Punjabis faced their new challenges boldly and with fortitude. They took any kind of work and business, and no one reduced themselves to begging. While the government went all out to establish refugee camps, and gave assistance to the extent possible, the Punjabi refugees established themselves and found their feet. Within a span of two years, they became the competitors of the local businessman. The great tragedy and devastation they had suffered not only did not demoralize them, but egged them on to greater endeavours in the new lands and surroundings.

The rehabilitation and restoration of the morale and confidence of the Muslim population was important too. Many had prepared to migrate, and were fear-stricken and often housed in camps for protection. The contribution of Pandit Rameshwar Dayal, the Collector of Saharanpur, is worth mentioning here. But for him most Muslims would have migrated and left Saharanpur. Rameshwar Dayal was a devout Hindu, and dressed exactly like Pandit Madan Mohan Malviya with his characteristic pugree, achkan, churidar, a scarf and a tilak on his forehead. While I have met many Hindu saints and scholars at his house in Saharanpur and Delhi, he was also most well read in Islamic lore and scriptures. He had an abiding love of Muslim culture and understood the Muslim mind and traditions with deep sympathy. He curbed and restrained the violence of the Hindu refugees with a heavy and unwavering hand.

I must also make mention here of Jamshed Ali Khan who was Chairman, Municipal Board, Saharanpur. A man not more than forty-eight years then, coming from an old Muslim family of tradition and culture, he had acquired the complete confidence of the Hindu refugee population and had a lot of influence on them. Whenever some administrative difficulties arose with the refugees in 1948 and 1949, it was Jamshed Ali Khan who resolved it.

Another event of significance that occurred when I was in Saharanpur was the assassination of Mahatma Gandhi. The news was received around 5.30 p.m. on 30 January 1948. It was dark, and the sky was cloudy. A fast and cold wind was blowing. We announced on loudspeakers in various parts of the city and the rural areas that Mahatma Gandhi had been shot dead by a Hindu. If this announcement had been delayed, and rumours allowed to spread, anything might have happened within minutes in this town teeming with refugees and Muslims.

The news was too shocking. The shooting of the apostle of non-violence, the saint of Sabarmati, the lone traveller who restored peace to Noakhali, who had led Indians from 1919—it was much too overwhelming. Undoubtedly, this sacrifice made many Hindus stop and reflect, and was the greatest factor in restoring security to the Muslims.

Another incident which stands out in my mind about Saharanpur is the RSS agitation in 1948-49. The organization, in the wake of Gandhiji's assassination, had been declared unlawful. Large-scale agitations and demonstrations were being held and many arrests followed. The number of prisoners in the jail here had gone to about 700 whereas the capacity of the District Jail was only 300. So it was decided to transfer about 400 prisoners to Bareilly Central Jail. The District Magistrate, B.P. Sahi, the SP L.B. Baijal and I, with a large police contingent went to force these RSS prisoners to come out from the barracks where they were clinging to one another to prevent being forced out. A constable was injured and a lathi charge followed. Thus they were sent to Bareilly. After a month, the number again went up, necessitating the dispatch of another 200 to Bareilly. They again adopted the same recalcitrant attitude and held forth in barracks clinging to each other. I was busy negotiating a settlement in the Imperial Tobacco factory and arrived on the scene inside the jail around 8 p.m., by which time the District Magistrate and SP had lined up the contingent of lathi-armed constables to force them out under a lathi charge.

I still vividly recall the scene. Deep inside the jail, after crossing two courtyards, there where the four barracks full of the young RSS prisoners, mostly lads shouting menacingly. As the prisoners and police faced each other I arrived, and asked the District Magistrate and SP to go home and that the matter would be handled by me. Already tired, they looked at me with some disbelief but left. Then to the dismay of the Deputy SP, and in the full view and hearing of all the prisoners, I asked him to go out of the jail too with every single policeman. Though unwilling initially, he finally marched out with his entire force. I had the door of the courtyard locked to prevent them from coming back. The only persons besides the 500 prisoners, now within the courtyard, were myself and the four jail wardens. In a moment of flash decision, I walked alone into the barracks in the midst of the boys shouting the slogans.

A hush fell, as I told them that most of them had been sentenced to jail by me, and that I was now alone in their midst, and they could manhandle me. I said I had dealt with the Congress Movement in 1942 also, but they had defied jail rules only when some principle or cause was involved. I showed them they were being simply unreasonable when accommodation for only 300 existed. They understood. Many of them gave me messages for their parents at home and so forth, but they came out on their own, and allowed themselves to be taken away.

I am relating this incident merely to show that though my action was bold and could be called foolhardy, one always has to assess the crowd in such situations and work to avoid unseemly violence. In any case, I got that inspiration on the spur of the moment and acted accordingly. I am proud of my handling of the situation that way.

In March 1948, one morning at 9 a.m., I drove in my car along the Canal Road to a village named Teetron in the interiors, about 50 km from Saharanpur. Somewhere on the kutcha road, the spring of my car broke. I walked to the village and sent a mechanic with my peon, but it could not be repaired till the evening. So the village chowkidar was left in charge and the peon also came away. I slept in the village that night. In the morning, I got up early and went in a bullock-drawn cart, locally called lahroo, to inspect the damage done to crops in several villages by a recent hailstorm. I returned at about noon. In the meanwhile, things had happened. My wife, alarmed when I did not return in the night, took a jeep provided by the District Magistrate and came to the spot where the car had broken down. To her horror, she found that the car was totally burnt out by a fire which had started nearby. However, she soon learnt that I was safe and in the village. About 5 p.m. that evening, we left in a jeep and reached the spot of the burnt-out car. At exactly the same spot, the jeep too broke down. So we had to leave it there and come back to the village on foot. Now we engaged a lahroo and went to Gangoh town, from where the pucca road runs to Saharanpur and where transport could be had.

It was a journey of nearly 20 km in a bullock cart on kutcha roads. It was just the two of us under a clear moonlit sky with stars shining mischievously in the heavens. It was somewhat chilly, and everything lay still in folds of darkness. It was like a magical journey for us amidst the peace of tranquil villages and hamlets along the route. We reached Gangoh around 11 p.m. and managed to get a place in a truck. When we had travelled some distance, a police search car came from the direction of Saharanpur and picked us up. Several search parties had gone around, thinking we were in trouble. But to this day the journey under the starlit sky as the lahroo jogged along with tinkling bells around the bullocks' necks, as the fresh air enlivened us, stands out in my mind.

Gangoh is a very ancient town with a large Muslim population. It had many Muslim saints of the Sufi sect, who have written and composed in the inimitable Hindi or Hindwi style of the local language. They have sung of the one benevolvent God who shines forth through all men and creatures and every little blade of grass. These Sufi saints of Gangoh are from the line of Khwaja Nizamuddin of Delhi.

At Saharanpur itself, I noticed the fall from the pedestal of many Congressmen who had earlier excelled in the national movement. They fell and have gone on falling ever since. I wish the Congress had disbanded itself in 1947, and regrouped into a new party. Then the members would not have asked for a price for their patriotism and demanded a share in the spoils. All kinds of people fished in the troubled waters. In 1948, the government referred a case to the District Magistrate of Saharanpur for his comments. The applicant, whom I called in court, had made out a case for a political pension on three counts:

1. That he had lost his job in the national movement.
2. That he had lost all his property in the movement.
3. That he had nothing to fall back upon.

I took his statement on oath and on cross-examination his case on each claim was as follows:

1. That he had been promised a sub-inspector's job by R.N. Marshsmith, SP, but on account of his nationalist views was not given the job in the 1930s.
2. That his father had deprived him of his share in property and given it to his brothers, because of his nationalist views.
3. That he and his wife were schoolteachers, but the salary was not sufficient and they had no offspring to fall back upon.

I reported to the government accordingly, but due to various pulls and pressures he was sanctioned the pension.

In another case, a friend of mine (I will not name him) was a Recruiting Officer for the army in 1942-46. When the war came to an end, his job also ended. He secured a certificate from the President, District Congress Committee, that he had been a sufferer in the Quit India Movement and so he was appointed a teacher in a government school in Meerut. He retired with pension.

Thus the political morals have continued to fall. And we have all fallen low indeed. We Indians boast about Gandhiji, Subhash Chandra Bose, Pandit Nehru and those others who suffered at the gallows with a smile on their faces during the national movement. Today when the old guard is no more, politicians of all colours are vying with each other across the country in perfidy, brigandage, sectarianism and plumbing the depths of human degradation.

8

In 1949, I was posted as Home Secretary to Delhi. Between 1949 to 1971 when I retired, I remained for seventeen years in Delhi and about six years at Allahabad. The history of this period is too close to us. It is not possible to hazard one's views on issues on which much greater authorities have been writing and analyzing. But during these thirty-two years, in my various assignments at the Centre and state, certain incidents stand out in my mind which are not likely to find mention in more erudite narratives, and which are peculiar to the period.

Delhi in 1948-49 was a much smaller city. The main area of New Delhi Municipal Committee was there but no colonies had been built or contemplated yet. The refugees were concentrated in Purana Qila. Their onrush posed a threat to the Muslim population, and hence the Deputy Commissioner of Delhi was obtained from UP, namely Pandit Rameshwar Dayal, and the Chief Commissioner was

Shanker Prasad. The civil services had shrunk due to the migration of the Muslim officers. About 2,000 policemen from UP were called in to Delhi as the entire police force of Delhi had to be built up again.

The city looked and felt so different from what it is now. The main hotels of importance during those days were the Imperial in New Delhi and the Maidens Hotel. They still had the old imperial atmosphere. New year's eve, New Year and Christmas Eve were celebrated with great gusto. The Oberoi International and other modern hotels did not exist then. Mehrauli was still the old town and Qutab Minar and its surroundings were reached through hills and jungles. It was not safe to travel after sunset. Some refugee shopkeepers had set up excellent dhabas at India Gate. Delhi thus had an old-world atmosphere, and the ravages of populist democracy had not yet been wrought on the face of the serene capital of a hundred years. Here, Sardar Patel was the ruling deity though Pandit Nehru was the Prime Minister. Others have written volumes on Sardar Patel, but what I saw in Delhi was the great awe which Sardar inspired at the time. It was said that if Sardar happened to be in the capital, all government servants attended office punctually at 10 a.m.

I am narrating a case concerning Sardar Baldev Singh which I dealt with as Home Secretary. The Defence Minister Sardar Baldev Singh was a great shikari and sent his arms licence for renewal to the District Magistrate with instructions that the quantity may be made unlimited. The District Magistrate Pandit Rameshwar Dayal increased the quantity of ammunition to 10,000, as under the Arms Act Rules it had to be a specified quantity, and returned the licence. Mr Vohra of the ICS, who was private secretary to the Defence Minister, returned it saying that the Hon'ble Minister desired it to be made unlimited and that the same had been done in 1934 in the case of one Chakraverty. The DM pointed out his difficulty, and also added that the case of Mr Chakraverty had been corrected. But the Defence Minister refused to relent, and desired that it must be made unlimited. The case was then referred to me as Home Secretary. I examined it and referred to the Chief Commissioner who wrote a very courteous note, explaining the difficulties of the administration and also requesting the minister to release our embarrassment. That note I sent to Vohra at 11.30 a.m. and requested him on the phone that this be placed before the minster. Vohra rang me back in an hour and said that the minister was annoyed, and desired that ammunition should be completely deleted and he would not relent on his demand. After consulting with Mr Shanker Prasad, I conveyed to Vohra that in that case the Chief Commissioner would be meeting Sardar Patel this evening along with the file. Within fifteen minutes came Vohra's call that the minister expressed his regret, and was withdrawing his demand, that the Chief Commissioner must not meet Sardar Patel about it, and that he accepted the renewed licence and the matter may be closed. This was the fear and awe for Sardar Patel which kept everybody in line.

I recall having seen the processions and receptions in honour of Bulganin and Khrushchev in 1955. There were great crowds and big ovations. At President's House Kumari Chandralekha Patel gave a brilliant Bharatanatyam performance. I also had the privilege of seeing Juthika Ray and hearing her sonorous voice.

The description of Delhi of those times would not be complete without mention of the poet Josh Malihabadi who constituted an integral part of Delhi till he migrated to Pakistan in 1956. Undoubtedly the greatest living Urdu poet of the subcontinent, he was highly respected by Prime Minister Nehru and had unfettered access to the Prime Minister's Teen Murti house. Josh Saheb was highly valued by the Chief Commissioner Shanker Prasad and Kunwar Mohinder Singh Bedi, himself an Urdu poet and convener and president of the mushiaras in India. Another great friend of Josh Malihabadi was Dr S.K. Saxena, a professor of philosophy and Deputy Director in the Publications Division. To enable Josh Saheb to augment his income, he was appointed editor of the *Aajkal* magazine of the Publications Division. Many a bar and restaurant of Delhi considered it an honour to cater to the needs of Josh Saheb. On his usual rounds early in the morning he used to drop into my house.

In 1951, Josh Saheb once came to see me in my office and made a request that since he was leaving for Bombay he needed a permit to carry twelve bottles of whisky. As Bombay was under Prohibition, I did not know how to help him, and there was no time either, as he was leaving within two days. So I wrote out an official letter to the Government of Bombay to the effect that Josh Malihabadi was coming with twelve bottles, being an addict, and that the possession may be regularized in Bombay. Within four days I received an express letter that it was not possible under the Bombay laws, and so Josh Saheb may be requested to not bring the bottles. I replied that Josh Saheb had since left for Bombay. The reply came that I should inform them of Josh Saheb's address in Bombay. I wrote back in due course that Josh Saheb had already returned.

Another incident involving Josh Saheb happened in 1951. Accompanied by Dr S.K. Saxena, Josh Saheb, around 5 p.m. in the evening, took his bottle of whisky, soda and glasses and parked his car in the Qudsia Garden. Here, in a lush green area, they spread out a neat bedsheet, put their whisky and glasses and both started their drinks, greatly satisfied and happy at the surrounding greenery, the trees and flowers. Meanwhile, a police constable arrived and told these happy gentlemen that Qudsia Garden was a public place, that they had committed an offence by drinking there. They would have to accompany him to the Kashmere Gate Police Station. Unperturbed, Josh Saheb tried to show the constable how poetic and entrancing the surroundings were, how extremely suitable for a drink, and the constable should come, sit and have a drink. The custodian of law politely refused the offer and insisted on the gentlemen accompanying him to the police station. Now Dr S.K. Saxena pleaded with the constable that Josh Saheb was an eminent man and a great friend of the Chief Commissioner and that he should ignore him. The constable thought that lest he be accused of neglecting his duty in such a case, he had to insist on their accompanying him to the police station. So, greatly disappointed at the unpoetic attitude of the constable, Josh Saheb and Dr Saxena packed up their things into the car, and drove towards Kashmere Gate. As soon as he got a chance, Josh Saheb sped to the residence of Mohinder Singh Bedi instead of the police station. As Bedi was not at his house, and as they did not find me either, they drove to the Chief Commissioner's house who settled the matter to their satisfaction and relief.

Another incident related to me personally. Josh Saheb was an atheist, and in his conversations used to say that man had created God in his own image. He always made fun of people doing puja or namaaz and used to say it was most degrading to prostrate oneself before an image of one's own creation. One morning some time in 1951, around 9 a.m., he came to my house. I was in the puja room, and then went for my breakfast. Some others also had come to see me and were waiting in the lawn. Josh Saheb was announced to me and I asked my man to bring him at the dining table. Josh Saheb came and sat with a very grave face. I offered him tea, but he declined saying his heart was heavy. When I asked him what was the matter, he asked me in turn if I paid my servant properly. I said I did, so he asked should a servant not safeguard the honour of his master. When I agreed, he told me that my servant had, in the presence of a number of persons waiting outside, said that Varma Saheb, namely myself, was doing puja. How could he have announced that a man in his proper senses and a respectable man at that was doing puja! My prestige had greatly suffered, according to him. I apologized and insisted that he have tea, but he stoutly refused on the ground that his heart had become very heavy. When I went to see Shanker Prasad that day, he told me that Josh Saheb had been to him and complained that the Home Secretary had been caught red-handed that morning doing puja.

On another occasion that same year, Dr S.K. Saxena went to visit Josh Saheb and found him quite morose. On enquiry he said that his wife was going to Malihabad the next morning, and had for the fifth time given him a long sermon about not being wasteful, and telling him that various articles of food were in the storerooms, and that he must not hand over the keys to the servant, Akbar. Next morning around 10 a.m., Dr Saxena visited him again and found him greatly upset again. Josh Saheb told him that his wife had gone to Malihabad by the morning train. When Dr Saxena said he should not be so sad, they had been married for fifty years after all, Josh Saheb replied how while he was standing on the platform, all the time, his wife was delivering to him from the window of the compartment, her sermon about the things in the storeroom, and that he must not give the keys to Akbar. Dr Saxena bade him be cheerful, now that she was gone and asked him what he had done about her instructions. Josh Saheb said he had immediately handed over the keys to Akbar, but that he had simultaneously enjoined upon Akbar on the honour of a Muslim never to open the storeroom, and had given him money to buy things from the market for each day's consumption and to allow perishable things in the storeroom to rot, but not interfere with the lock of that room. Now he revealed the main cause of his discomfiture. Every year he himself used to go to Malihabad to sell his mango crop, and his custom was to sell it for Rs 5000 but show only Rs 3000 in the sale documents, and thereby save Rs 2000 for drinks. Now not only did he stand to lose those Rs 2000 but his wife would discover his yearly concealment of the money and he would have trouble on her return.

I remember a mushaira which took place in the Red Fort in 1950. Prime Minister Nehru was present. The poem recited by Josh Saheb was a superb one, but fiery and critical of the affairs of the country and the social structure. Next morning, Josh Saheb received a call from the Prime Minister's House and was certain he was to be given a reprimand. He was taken to the office where Pandit Nehru was busy with files. Panditji asked an orderly to call in his daughter, Mrs Indira Gandhi. According to Josh Saheb, he felt that the dressing down he was to receive was likely to be in the presence of the daughter. When finally Panditji was free from the files, and Indiraji had arrived, he asked Josh Saheb to recite the poem of the previous night. When he did so, Panditji told him what a superb poem it was, but that if he recited it again in public, he was likely to find himself a guest of Sardar Patel, meaning that the Home Minister might put him in jail for sedition.

Thus went about the life of Delhi. I met Josh Saheb in Karachi in 1958, shortly after he had migrated to Pakistan, and he was most unhappy and full of remembrances. One of his famous poems recited and quoted in Delhi in the post-Independence years was:

ہل چل روا، خروش روا، سنسنی روا

رشوت روا، فساد روا، رہزنی روا

القصہ ہر وہ شے کہ ہے ناکردنی روا

انسان کے لہو کو پیو اذنِ عام ہے

انگور کی شراب کا پینا حرام ہے

Vehshat rawa, inaad rawa, dushmani rawa
Hulchul rawa, kharosh rawa, sansani rawa
Rishwat rawa, fasaad rawa, rahzani rawa
Al qissa har vo shai ke hai na-kardani rawa
    Insaan ke lahu ko piyo, izn e aam hai
    Angoor ki sharaab ka peena haraam hai*

After the very first election in Delhi, a ministry was constituted in March 1952, and the Delhi State Assembly was inaugurated by Shanker Prasad. I was Secretary to the Constitutional Chief Commissioner. I recall when the Assembly was opened in the old historic Secretariat Assembly Hall, where the Central Legislative Assembly of

---

**Publisher's note*: Columnist and scholar Pervez Hoodbhoy translates these lines as: 'Insanity thrives, ill-will thrives, enmity thrives, chaos thrives, disorder thrives, rumouring thrives, bribery thrives, conflict thrives, theft thrives. In short, all that is bad does so splendidly well. Drink the blood of man and it matters but little. Drink wine from the grape and you are damned till eternity.' (Pervez Hoodbhoy, 'South Asia's Apostle of Secular Humanism: Josh Malihabadi', newageislam.com)

the Viceroy and Governor General used to meet in 1920s and '30s. Vallabhbhai Patel as speaker thundered, and Pandit Madan Mohan Malviya spoke in his sonorous voice. The experiment, inaugurated with so much pomp and fanfare, crumbled after about six years. The diarchic system was unworkable. In my opinion, Delhi must not have a separate legislature and ministry.

In 1953 Chou En-lai, the Chinese Premier, visited and I shook hands with him along with other officers of the Delhi government. Delhi was aflame with 'Hindi Chini Bhai Bhai' slogans. Who thought then of the perfidy of 1962.

When I was Home Secretary, Delhi State, the Health Ministry under the Health Minister Raj Kumari Amrit Kaur organized a lottery for sale of a tractor to one lucky ticket holder in an exhibition to be held in the Ramlila Grounds. Lottery was an offence under the law at the time. When it dawned on the officers of the Health Ministry that it was an offence, they asked me for permission, which, I wrote back, could not be given. They then wrote to me that they had made an application earlier and that this could have been pointed out then, and that the sale of tickets had been done so now the lottery had to be gone through. They complained to the Home Ministry too. I explained to the Home Ministry that the existence of an earlier letter was fake, and that in any case an act that went against the law would be committed if the Health Ministry went through with the lottery. The file was put up to Rajaji, who was the Home Minister. He passed orders that should the Health Ministry proceed with the plan, the organizers and the minister would be prosecuted by the Delhi state authorities. The Health Ministry hastily cancelled the lottery. Such was the authority of Rajaji and the law at that time.

I would like to mention in some detail here about Mr Shanker Prasad who was Chief Commissioner of Delhi between 1948-54. He was a great administrator. The administration of Delhi was built up by him from almost scratch. Sardar Patel had charged him with the construction of the new Collectorate and the new jail. He saw to it that the foundations of both projects were laid in his time.

The construction of Tis Hazari Court has an interesting history. I took up the project from 1951 to 1952 but due to financial setbacks, it stalled. The Finance Ministry put a stop to it. When it was turned down in 1953 in a ministers' meeting at about 8 p.m., I reported this straight to Shanker Prasad. I told him that unless the project went through now, it had no chance in future as both of us might go away on transfer. The current court building then was at Kashmere Gate in an old and dilapidated building. He asked me to get it condemned by the CPWD, which was done. Then the third day, known only to me and the Deputy Commissioner, he brought Dr Katju, the Home Minister at around 11 a.m. to the courts, unannounced. It was crowded like a fish market, and the minister could not enter any court. He also saw the condition of the building. That same evening the project was sanctioned by the Finance Ministry. Tihar Jail, too, was sanctioned by the Finance Ministry, by some other stratagem. The introduction of sales tax, in 1951, was entirely due to the guidance given to me by Shanker Prasad, as also the reorganization of the Secretariat, the district and police administration.

I remember the case of an Assistant Sub-Inspector of Faiz Bazar police station who was not let down by Shanker Prasad despite pressure from the Prime Minister. The ASI had resisted the assault of one Gulap Chand Jain, treasurer of the city Congress. This person then complained to the PM. Shanker Prasad wrote beautiful notes to the Prime Minister, full of courtesy and consideration, explaining his point of view till the PM agreed.

The initial organization and integration of Indian Airlines was a stupendous task which only Shanker Prasad could achieve in record time. I had the honour of assisting him in the process for three to four years and watched him at work.

In the context of Indian Airlines, I would like to mention an incident at Karachi in 1957. One Narayanan was Station Manager at Karachi and a strike was in the offing, as the Pakistani employees were agitating and even canvassing against Indian Airlines. I reached Karachi, stayed in the High Commission, and met C.C. Desai, the High Commissioner. At the airline office I proceeded to meet individual employees. In between, the Joint Secretary and Vice President of the Union asked to see me and presented me with a list of their demands. I assured them that I would not leave Karachi till I had met their demands to their satisfaction.

During my meetings with each employee, I came to know that the President and Secretary of the Union were ill, one had a fracture. In the evening, I went to see each one of these two at their homes. They and their families were extremely delighted by the visit. I was with them each for over an hour, sanctioned medical expenses, and had tea offered by their families. When I finally reached the High Commission, it was around 10 p.m. It was January and cold and windy. I told the staff car driver to take the car to his house and come the next morning at 11 o'clock.

The next day, when I reached the office, the same Union representatives met me again, along with an application that in view of my sympathetic attitude they had withdrawn their demands and merely wanted me to look into their grievances. This happened again in a hostile Pakistan in 1958, when the employees took their case to the Labour Tribunal. I again went to Karachi. Immediately they put in an application to the court whose judge was from Lucknow that since I was there and since the employees had full confidence in me, they wanted me to adjudicate, to agree or disagree on each demand, and they would accept my decision. This has been mentioned by the judge in his award, a copy of which should be in the Indian Airlines office. I mention this because I have found that a touch of compassion makes even the most hostile person your kin. I reckon this as one of my proud achievements.

When I was in the Indian Airlines, I visited Kabul in 1956. We flew with Captain Huilgol as the pilot in a two-engine DC-3 Dakota. It was fascinating to see the rugged mountains of the North-west Frontier Province, the cliffs of Hindu Kush, and the Takhte Suleman from 15,000 feet in the air. We stayed in the best of hotels at the time for a mere 55 Afghanis per day. I also visited the tomb of the first Mughal emperor Babur, set in very simple surroundings. When on our way back we flew over the rugged mountain passes into the plains of Punjab, a panorama of green fields and flowing rivers opened up suddenly before our eyes. I was reminded of the great attraction India held for the invaders from Western Asia, the Greeks, the Huns and the Mongols. Inhabitants of those rugged inhospitable regions, they had heard of the vast riches of Hindustan, and when they reached, they must have been similarly struck with the beauty of the verdant plains and fields.

When I visited the grave of Bahadur Shah, the last

Mughal Emperor, I could imagine his anguish at his exile from Hindustan and from Delhi. When flying in a Dakota from Colombo, Sri Lanka, watching the sea below, I thought of the legendary bridge built by Lord Rama and the unsurpassed description of the seas in Sunder Kand of the Ramayana by Valmiki.

In 1968, I did a sea journey with my wife on a holiday trip. We travelled in a cabin from Bombay to Dwarka, the mythical abode of Lord Krishna. The morning broke as the temple of Somnath rose in the distance along the shore. From Dwarka we motored to Porbandar and passed through barren lands and salt manufacturing spots. The route is desolate, and I was reminded of the *Mahabharata* story that while Arjuna was returning from Dwarka, in these places wild tribes had plundered his caravan. At Porbandar we visited Gandhiji's house and saw the room where he was born. It was an unforgettable experience.

I was in Delhi for about seventeen years, first from 1949 to 1958, and then after a sojourn at Allahabad for a three-year term as Excise Commissioner, I was back to Delhi in 1961, first in the Agriculture Ministry and then as Joint Secretary, Ministry of Information and Broadcasting with additional charge as Director General, All India Radio (AIR) for a few months. I thus saw Delhi pass from its old moorings to the fast-changing modern face. Before 1954, Delhi stood almost static. Connaught Place was there, and the growing Janpath market, but Chandni Chowk was still the main market, though the tramcars were gone. Mehrauli still wore the veil of the Mughal times and Qutab Minar was an attraction for lazy Sunday visitors. The jungles and the hills along Mehrauli Road were untouched by the human hand of destruction and even wild animals abounded. Tughlakabad had the look of an abandoned capital.

The Ridge and the jungles along Delhi University were intact. It was in the cover of those ridges that Timur's armies lay hidden and camped before they fell on the Delhi of the Tughlaqs. The battle left the ground of Delhi soaked in human blood.

In the 1950s, Metcalfe House was there, where Sir Charles Metcalfe, the British Resident, once lived. This and Ludlow Castle lay along the present Raj Bhawan Marg in front of the Chief Commissioner's office. India Gate lay sprawling with the President's House, and the North Block and South Block, commanding a view of the princely houses at the lower level—Hyderabad House, Jaipur House, Baroda House and so on, almost like a modern version of a Mughal durbar. That's how Lutyens had designed it.

The villages around Mehrauli, about 252 of them, lay untouched by the depredations of the later years. The Yamuna river ran its course amidst bushes and jungles. The beautification of the bank had not commenced nor was the Ring Road there. The Jamuna Bazar, full of slums and hovels, was still there. In Chandni Chowk, the waterway had disappeared, as had the trams, but the bustle and the crowds were still the same. The famous kotwali of Mughal days was still there. Kashmere Gate, though crumbling, was there, as were Lahori Gate, Dilli Darwaza and the Khooni Darwaza. All these, together with some old families who continued to live there, were a link to a past that was gradually being forgotten.

Mohammad Omar was a tailor at Kashmere Gate who in 1950 still recalled the Viceroy. A descendant of the last Mughal king Bahadur Shah, one Mirza was posted as Assistant Superintendent in the Deputy Commissioner's office. The old Secretariat had an old-world character. Then, there was no mad rush, no din and bustle. The men and women of Delhi had some leisure. Pandit Nehru with his red rose could be seen in big Delhi celebrations or parties. Wherever he stood, the life and soul of India pulsated there.

9

The description of the old Delhi administration would not be complete without a mention of Dr Sushila Nayyar, the Health Minister of Delhi, 1952-54. A disciple of Mahatma Gandhi, and the author of *Karavas ki Kahani*—a record of Mahatma Gandhi's life in Yerwada jail—she was a great idealist, and an indefatigable worker. As minister, she wanted everything to be done quick, in no time, unmindful of the realities or the practical possibilities. Once when my colleague K.K. Sharma went on a month's leave, I held the additional charge of the Health portfolio. She called me and gave me a list of fourteen items which had to be completed in a fortnight. This included the construction of a ward in a hospital. She was, however, sincere and honest about everything, almost child-like in simplicity and outlook. She was sympathetic, but a hard taskmaster.

She had taken a special interest in the establishment and construction of a children's home. I had pursued it long and had had a grant sanctioned for a site where it exists even today. Dr Sushila Nayyar did not like the site, though it was not her portfolio, but a part of the reserved subject under the Home portfolio. She asked me to select another site. In January 1953, we were at a dinner party at 20, Alipore Road in honour of the visiting Home Minister of Vindhya Pradesh. It broke up around 11 p.m., and Dr Sushila Nayyar asked me to come to her residence at around 7 a.m. the next day so that she could go with me to inspect other possible sites. When I reached her house at 7 a.m., in the first fortnight of January 1953, it was dark and foggy. I, however, found that she had already been holding a meeting of officers since 6 a.m. When this meeting dispersed, she offered me coffee. I got round her by complimenting her on her energy and patriotism and expressed my concern at her health. I then persuaded her to abandon the wild goose chase of a site, lest the grant lapse. In that mood she agreed and I came home, relieved.

Here I would like to mention an incident which considerably agitated Delhi for a fortnight. It was the second marriage of the former Political Secretary of Sardar Patel, with a girl then working as a receptionist in the passport office of Delhi, which fell directly under me. This Secretary had been the most important civilian during Sardar Patel's time and his importance and reputation within and without the country back then was almost as great as the Sardar's. News of the planned marriage was conveyed to me first when the girl asked for leave on the 3rd of December, 1953. Having failed to persuade her to give up the plan, I conveyed the information to Shanker Prasad, who was a great friend of this secretary's. Then he and other civilians and relations used their powers of persuasion with the former political secretary, trying to dissuade him from bigamy, but to no purpose. The news even reached the Prime Minister and he was also opposed to the marriage. The government passed orders transferring the former secretary forthwith to Bombay where there was a law against bigamy. He resigned from the service, but then the government withdrew the order. Since I was known to both the secretary and the woman he wanted to marry, I was deputed to do my utmost to prevent the wedding. Now I was in the unenviable position of having to pass intelligence about the expected moves of the couple to Shanker Prasad and the authorities.

I recall how I was summoned at about 6 p.m. on 8 December 1953 before a war council in the then office of the Chief Controller of Imports and Exports where Shanker Prasad, K.B. Lal, V.P. Menon sat disheartened. They informed me that their efforts had broken down. Now I was asked to go to the girl's house, use my influence and remain there till the ceremonies started. At the bride's house, the marriage preparations were on, the flowers and the garlands had been arranged, food was being cooked, and the pandit was waiting. But the bridegroom, realizing my situation, out of sheer affection and consideration for me, cancelled the marriage for that day in Delhi. Later, on 10th December, both went away to Agra and married at Mathura. The event rocked Delhi at the time, and the civil services world stood shocked and dazed.

The second wife of the former political secretary passed away in 1966, and he himself finally retired as Defence Secretary. He was also Special Secretary in the Ministry of Food and Agriculture (where I worked with him), Director General Post and Telegraphs, and Chairman, Indian Airlines. He was a great admirer of Sardar Patel, and wrote about him. He was one of the three collaborators of Sardar Patel in the integration of states. He had a powerful memory, and wielded a formidable pen. He was a great administrator and also a compelling speaker and could speak on any subject without notice. A lover of Urdu literature, he was also a prominent figure in mushairas, along with Mohinder Singh Bedi. He and Josh Malihabadi got on famously.

After his second marriage, the services community kept aloof from him socially, though he continued to be kind to me and invited me to exclusive gatherings. He went on to become Secretary to Prime Minister Morarji Desai during the Janta Party rule. Sadly, his passing in 1981 went almost unmarked.

Readers of today may be interested to know how sales tax got introduced in Delhi. In the time of my predecessor, the Chief Minister of UP, Pandit Govind Ballabh Pant, wrote that there being no sales tax in Delhi was leading to loss of revenue. For a year the matter lay unattended. In August 1949, N.M. Patnaik, my predecessor, and Home and Revenue Secretary, handed over the file to me on his transfer. I treated it as an urgent matter, and immediately went through all the Sales Tax Acts and systems in the country by reading up on the subject. In consultation with P.M. Basu, Deputy Secretary Finances, I decided upon applying the single point tax system of the West Bengal Sales Tax Act, with copious borrowings from the UP Sales Tax exemptions. Having framed the proposals and the modifications in the Act, I had it approved by the Advisory Council to the Chief Commissioner and by October 1949 had it sent to the Government of India.

As Sardar Patel was not well disposed towards sales tax in Delhi, the proposal lay dormant in the Home and Finance Ministry for the whole of 1950. Only a question was asked as to what was likely to be the revenue, to which, by a rough calculation, I indicated the figure of one crore in the first year. Sardar Patel died in December 1950. In the budget proposals of 1951, Finance Minister C.D. Deshmukh announced inclusion of a revenue of one crore from sales tax in Delhi. In 1951, I worked out and set up the machinery. It has been a source of great satisfaction that the sales tax revenue of Delhi during the first year (1951-52) came to one crore and five lakhs.

When I was in the Indian Airlines, there occurred an incident worth mentioning. One Dr Aijaz Hussain of the Educational Service of UP was on some sort of deputation in the Middle East. He sent by air, a hookah made of glass as a gift to Dr Sampurnanand, Chief Minister of UP. Dr Sampurnanand and his Secretary, S.S.L. Kakkar, asked the Station Manager of Indian Airlines, Lucknow, to collect it. This small cargo though somehow flew to Calcutta from where it was flown to Lucknow. The customs authorities valued it at Rs 100 and added cent per cent duty. To this Indian Airlines added about Rs 50 as air freight. So a bill of about Rs 250 was sent to Dr Sampurnanand. There was no response from the Chief Minister's house despite a great deal of correspondence. Then the Chief Traffic Manager, Indian Airlines at the headquarters in Delhi, took it up without any success. The matter came to me. The Chairman, Shanker Prasad, had the hookah summoned to his office to examine what it was like. It was a small glass object, costing in my opinion, not more than Rs 25. We wondered how the customs could have priced it at Rs 100. So Shanker Prasad had an idea. He asked me to make a present of it to the Chairman, Central Board of Revenue, since Dr Sampurnanand was not interested.

I drew up a note on the above lines and concluded by saying that Indian Airlines had the greatest pleasure in presenting it to the Chairman, Central Board of Revenue. I took the note and the hookah to A.K. Roy, the Chairman, at his office in North Block and made a formal presentation. He was taken aback and asked me what should be the price. We agreed that the price should not exceed Rs 25. So he fixed the price at Rs 25 and thus the hookah was to cost Rs 50. A few days later I went to Lucknow, met the Chief Minister, related to him the whole incident and submitted that the Indian Airlines would be happy to present it to the Chief Minister. He did not agree. He said that the Indian Airlines was a public organization and payment must be made. So he accepted the hookah and gave me a cheque for Rs 50 and the air freight.

I may mention that when I was at Jerusalem in 1962, I enquired the price of such a hookah available in the market there. I felt satisfied that the price was around 25 Indian rupees.

10

I was Excise Commissioner, UP for three years, from 1958 to 1961, and had an opportunity to travel the length and breadth of the state and watch the working of the government. A memorable journey was to Badrinath, in particular the journey on foot from Joshimath. The charm of travelling on foot cannot be felt now. In fact, there is nothing like walking on foot in these areas. One wonders what the land was like when Sri Shankaracharya would have travelled the length and breadth of this vast country on foot, in the 8th century, when industrialization had not disfigured the faces of hills and mountains, and when rivers and forests existed in their splendour. Now commercialisation has made Haridwar crowded, and at Rishikesh numerous buildings have sprung up. Some so-called yogis have set up air-conditioned ashrams, where you meet more materialism than spiritualism. Most of the mahants of these ashrams measure their greatness by the wealth and ostentatiousness of their ashram, and by the number of great and powerful men and foreigners in their following.

Austere living combined with spiritual striving was the hallmark of our ancient rishis, and it is this spiritual heritage on which India takes its pride amongst the nations of the world. Swami Vivekanand was an example, as was Gandhiji. I have no doubt, however, that this sweep of materialism will be halted by an upsurge of spiritual fervour in this land of Gautam Buddha.

As Excise Commissioner, I attended a conference at Udaipur in Rajasthan and had an occasion to visit the fort of Chittor. Apart from other historical sites, I also saw the place where Rani Padmini and other Rajput women had thrown themselves in the vast funeral pyre, as the men went down fighting in the battlefield. I stood awestruck, as the ashes mixed with small bones are still lying there. I collected a bagful, brought it to Allahabad, and poured it into the waters at the holy confluence of the Ganga and Yamuna. That is the only thing I felt I could do, though these ashes and bones constituted in themselves the holiest and most sanctified remains of those immortal souls. At Udaipur, I saw the great painting of Rana Pratap holding the head of his loyal horse Chetak, as the dying horse casts a last longing look at his master.

On a visit to Bhubaneshwar in Odisha, I stayed at

the inspection house at Udayagiri about 11 km from Bhubaneshwar. I had a close view of the Udayagiri caves and stone engravings and figures dating to the 3rd century BC.

I have visited almost all the districts of UP. Of these, the most rewarding was visiting the district of Almora, and seeing not only picturesque places of scenic beauty, but also the old temples and to go up the hill to visit the temple of Bharamari Devi.

Dr Sampurnanand was the Chief Minister, a man known for his integrity. He was outstanding, though his ministers were nowhere of his calibre. The Congress party was not a divided house then. Pandit Nehru was the Prime Minister, and like the sun, gave his attention equally to all the states. Dissidence or indiscipline were not there. Hence the government had authority and its writ ran everywhere. As Excise Commissioner, I noticed a tendency amongst the MLAs to pester and persecute ministers about postings and transfers. As many MLAs came from the villages, they were interested in the posting and transfer of Constables, Sub-Inspectors of Police, Excise Inspectors and so forth. But by and large, the civil servant could tender advice freely and get his point of view accepted, and prevent misuse of authority.

The functioning of parliamentary democracy was on the decline. In 1959 or 1960, the excise budget was being introduced for the next year. Dr Sita Ram was the minister in charge of Excise. I was present in the official gallery to assist the minister by supplying answers to points raised by the opposition. The budget was introduced. Raj Narain Singh, MLA, stood up to comment on the budget introduced by 'the Harijan Minister of Excise'. This word offended Dr Sita Ram, who objected. Raj Narain Singh persisted, and so for half an hour there were abuses and counterabuses and complete rowdyism in the Assembly. By then the time allotted to the budget was over and it was declared passed. Thus democracy triumphed and the rule of the people by the people was upheld, and the greatness of the Indian Constitution maintained. Now such a thing is the order of the day in Assemblies and the Parliament.

11

From 1961 to 1964 I was Extension Commissioner, Ministry of Food and Agriculture. I had been called to the ministry from UP to deal with the Agricultural District Programme, popularly known as the package programme. It was in collaboration with the Ford Foundation who had provided eight experts to collaborate with eight Indian experts.

I noticed, by 1962, that the American team wanted to dominate and make contacts with the district staff in the states independently of the ministry. The head of the foundation was Dr Ensminger who wielded considerable influence with ministers, and was in a position to dictate to senior officers in the ministries. These experts had full knowledge of all the files and their contents, and were even influencing policy notings and decisions. They used to get round some officers and staff by providing them with trips abroad on training pretexts. Their devious ways and some undesirable contacts in the states amongst the project staff came to my notice, and so I wrote a letter to the head of the Ford Foundation team that they must not go to the districts except under a programme approved by me and along with their Indian counterparts. Within two days the package programme part of my extension work was taken away from me and given to a more pliable officer. Such was the sinister influence of the Americans in those days. They gave aid and yet were hated. In 1962, when I was in Jerusalem, the common view among all the delegates from Asian and Middle Eastern countries in private conversation was hatred of these aid-giving arrogant Americans.

Here I may say a few words about the package programme. The programme sought to make a breakthrough in agriculture under the direction and control of the Collector, but also under the directions of a project officer. It was a step in the right direction. There was also a German package programme in agriculture in Mandi district in Himachal Pradesh, and a Japanese programme in paddy cultivation in West Bengal. In the latter two programmes, the Germans and the Japanese were down-to-earth realists and worked with hands in the field, forcing our specialists to climb down to the fields. The Americans did more of talking and advising.

In March 1962, I visited Jerusalem for a conference.

The agricultural programmes there bore no comparison to the vast agricultural effort in our country. On this trip I got to see many important sites, like the Church of Nativity and the river Jordan, which appeared so much smaller than our mighty rivers. The Dead Sea was another sight. The Arab officers were most hospitable. In the market where I bought something, the lady of the shop reduced the price because, she said, I came from the land of Nehru.

The Agriculture Ministry experience was most fascinating. I visited most of the agriculture colleges and universities. At the vast campus of Coimbatore college, I was most impressed by the teaching as well as the farming. The Home Science College of Dr Devadas struck me as being run on most sound lines. Padma Shri G.D. Naidu of Coimbatore invited me to his house. The saga of his rise from a truck driver to a great industrialist and farmer is the story of a self-made man who retained his sweet temperament and sense of honour. He showed me round his watch factory and his farm. In Tamil Nadu, I found a very high level of farming in Tanjore district. In East Godavari district of Andhra Pradesh, I came across a farmer with 10 acres of land who had an air-conditioned house. I also visited the grape orchard of Dr Koteshwar Rao whose example prompted me to extend perlett variety of grape cultivation around Delhi. I felt unhappy at the poor performance of agriculture in Assam. Ludhiana's agriculturists were superb with their application, industry and physique, but the western UP farmer was no inferior either, and the farmers in Tanjore and East Godavari with their comparatively small farms were no less efficient.

In Jalgaon district, I stayed as a guest of a cooperative society where a great farmer, a Patel, took me to a field. He told me that the field in question lay barren and saline due to water seepage from underneath, and that agriculture specialists and experts had been unable to reclaim it. On his own initiative he had dug a broad deep well with the result that all the underground seepage was diverted to the well and the land got reclaimed. Now he had been using the well for irrigation of the same field which had an abundant wheat crop.

I was thrilled to see the rich sugarcane harvest in the fields of the Minister of Agriculture A.P. Sinde. At Nashik I found intensive district programmes in agriculture being pursued and implemented at the ground level. I also visited most of the states as a member of the Cooperative Credit Panel of the Planning Commission headed by B.P. Patel, Secretary, Community Development. I also visited several states as member of a panel to make recommendations for development of agriculture. I recall that in one of our visits to a village about 40 km from Bhopal, we came across an irrigation tank. All the tenants complained of poor production. In their midst was a Punjabi refugee cultivator who sought a separate interview and told us confidentially that his field yielded much more as a result of his improved system and supervision, but that to divulge it would be inviting trouble from thieves and dacoits!

One of the firm recommendations we made in Bihar was to break up the too large districts which were formerly fashioned on the basis of the Permanent Settlement of Lord Cornwallis.

In Gujarat, I visited Baroda where I gave a talk at the university. Undoubtedly Baroda is an extremely neat and orderly town and speaks of the efficiency of the Gaekwad administration. The agriculture college at Anand was outstanding.

I will not dwell on the scenic aspects of Kashmir, the paradise of the world. I visited the spots chronicled in tourist maps and in writings and books dating from the time of Emperor Jahangir. In enforcing the package programme in Kashmir, I encountered difficulties. The Agriculture Minister diverted funds and vehicles to areas other than agriculture and would not reply to letters from the ministry. Ultimately, I had to request the Accountant General to stop payments. This made the Agriculture Minister sit up and become more agriculture minded.

Sikkim in 1964 was still under the Chogyal. I visited him and the monasteries. Agriculture here leaned towards horticulture and hill cultivation. Gangtok was a small town.

Kalimpong was fascinating with its scenic beauty, and developed terrace cultivation.

In Himachal Pradesh, it was interesting to see apple orchards on the way from Kulu to Mandi, as orange-red apples hung in clusters in the overhanging branches. The lilting and falling waters of Sutlej as they move along singing a perpetual melody are unforgettable when one stays the night at Katrian Inspection House.

I also recall my visit to Trivandrum. The district of Aleppey was performing very well. In this connection, I visited Kanyakumari. I had visited it earlier in 1957 also. I reached the PWD Inspection House on the shore and was able to take a picture of the red ball of the sun in the evening, as the rim dipped into the Arabian Sea. Next morning, I was fortunate to get a clear picture of the rising sun in the Indian Ocean. Bathing at the junction of the oceans was an experience. The Vivekanand Memorial structure had not come up, and the bare rock stood majestic in the Indian Ocean untouched by the intruding hand of man.

This opportunity that I got to traverse the agricultural fields all over the country, stretching from the green paddy fields in Tanjore, to the vast sugarcane and banana-studded stretches of Andhra Pradesh; the forest wealth of Madhya Pradesh, and the gold and green areas in UP and Bihar showed me so many different aspects of India. I have broken bread with the rugged cultivator in Rajasthan. I have been charmed at the scenic beauties surrounding the rich paddy fields in the terraces of the hills and mountains of Jammu and Kashmir. The vast panorama of this land of ours lies spread like a multicoloured carpet, as men and women work and toil in fields and forests.

12

In 1964, I was transferred to the Ministry of Information and Broadcasting as Joint Secretary. I was put in charge of All India Radio and Television, and other information departments. It is a fascinating ministry with a cultural atmosphere, where talent and intellect are most prized. With my literary background and an inclination towards music and art, I felt greatly satisfied. There I was in the midst of scholars, artists and writers of repute. I also realized that publicity was most essential for the government. The Ministry of Information and Broadcasting has a seasoned officer of the Central Information Service as Adviser in each ministry. Through this officer, the ministry has a knowledge of the working of each minister. Through the Press Information Officer a great deal of control is exercised on what is to be published in newspapers. The Publications Division is an establishment of scholars; it also keeps contact with eminent writers of repute. The All India Radio (AIR) is a home of reputed artists and is in contact with artists and musicians all over the country. AIR can take pride in having nurtured great musicians like Bismillah Khan, and luminaries like Begum Akhtar and M.S. Subbulakshmi. There are a host of writers, poets and musicians who sat and are still sitting in that dome of learning at Parliament Street. The Station Directors of AIR in various state capitals have been people of merit, who awakened the literary and musical talents in the states. I had the opportunity to meet a great many of them.

In AIR thousands of tapes are lying unused. They contain all the music and heritage of India. They are invaluable and can be converted into gold by collaborating with some company to make records of them. I had embarked on this project and had held discussions with some companies when I left the ministry in 1968.

AIR is a big organization with a large number of staff artists of all categories. In addition, there is an administrative army to run it. Each wing in the AIR considers the other less important and no one wing is willing to work in subordination to the other. It has, therefore, been found necessary to have an IAS officer at the head as Director General. But whenever an officer has headed the organization, trouble has ensued and led to indiscipline and bickering. The main aim of the Director General is to weld together the disparate elements into a harmonious whole and to be strict in administration and discipline. Hence in my opinion, it is only an IAS officer with an artistic and literary bent and a top administrator who should be at the head of this august organization.

In addition to being Joint Secretary in the ministry for about six months, I was also Director General, All India Radio. I had thus the privilege of having had close association with the artists of AIR in Delhi and outside. The staff artists with all their talent are not valued as they are not government servants. I had the feeling that these poor staff artists, specially the writers, the musicians and the instrumentalists are viewed as hired labour by the Programme Officers who are in command at the headquarters and at the AIR stations. While their image in public is high, they are not given their due within the organization. Efforts should be made to build up their image and accord to them a status and respectability without making them government servants, as this would cause degeneration in quality.

I take credit for having introduced farm broadcasting on AIR as I had come from the Ministry of Food and Agriculture with ideas full of farming.

I was also responsible for negotiating with the Germans, signing an agreement and setting up the regular television station with German equipment. Till then, the Delhi television station broadcast educational programmes on equipment given by the Ford Foundation. I also negotiated with the Russians and with Yugoslavia for setting up high-powered medium wave transmitters. The Indian Institute of Mass Communication was set up in my time. I also had a hand in fighting Pakistani propaganda through AIR and other media during the 1965 war with Pakistan. I had it from authoritative sources in UK, Canada and Europe that AIR had a reputation for veracity.

When I was DG, AIR, one day I had a file regarding a certain matter concerning the instrumentalists in AIR. There was a recommendation and I had to pass the orders. Before doing so, I directed Chaturlal, the famous tabla player, be asked to come up to my room. Chaturlal came up. The DG's room is big, well-furnished and impressive. He was slightly nervous. I asked Chaturlal to sit down and offered him a chair. I told him that I had called him to elicit his opinion on that particular matter. At this, Chaturlal broke into tears and wept loudly. When I asked him what the matter was, he told me that during the many years that he had been in the AIR, he had never seen the Director General and had never been called to his room and such an honour of consultation had never been conferred on him. Chaturlal is no more, but the scene still comes alive for me today.

Another time, as Director General, I had issued a circular that any employee of the AIR wishing to meet me could do so between 5 p.m. and 6 p.m. It was intended for the staff in Delhi. One day, between 5 and 6 p.m., a Programme Executive from Hyderabad sent his card in. I enquired whether he had come from Hyderabad just to see me. When he said yes, I asked him why. He said that for some years he had been making a representation about his seniority and that no reply had been given and that he had been smarting under a sense of great injustice. First I asked if he knew any officer in the DG's office in whom he had complete trust. He named one person.

I called the officer he had named and asked the Deputy Director (Administration) to hand over the file to this officer. I told them to come to me the third day at 5 p.m. On the third day, when all three came to my room, I was most pleasantly surprised when this Programme Executive told me that he was now absolutely satisfied that no injustice had been done to him. I asked him to go and work now wholeheartedly and that I had no doubt that this time he would earn a good report. Thus his misery ended, merely because he had been shown his case. I have always been of the opinion that establishment matters relating to individual employees must not be kept secret from the person affected. There is nothing secret about it and a government servant must know. It is the secrecy and hush hush attitude that causes hardship.

Another time, Begum Akhtar came to my house in

Pandara Park and told me that I should look into the case of one Mr Khan, as she felt that an injustice had been done to him since 1953. I asked my Deputy Secretary B.S. Dashratty and Under Secretary J.D. Jain to put up the file. They told me that this case had been examined several times by several secretaries and all the ministers since 1953, and had been rightly turned down. I asked them to leave the file for my examination. I found this one was also like the one of the Programme Executive of Hyderabad. Mr Khan was the Station Director of Radio Station, Hyderabad State when Hyderabad was merged with the Indian union after police action in 1949. After that the work of integrating the staff started. This man was given the rank of a Programme Assistant in view of his payscale which was not comparable to the pay of a higher post in India. He used to have a position in the Hyderabad durbar, and had his perks and privileges. He used to be the highest officer of the radio station. So he was frustrated and started making representation after representation which were all rejected. In the process he became sour, unruly and disgruntled and earned adverse annual entries.

I had experience of a similar situation in 1954-58 when I had to do the integration of various categories of staff of the airline companies into one Integrated Airline Cadre. Positions previously held had been given importance. Therefore I felt that the man had been unfairly treated and his career had suffered. I explained this to the Deputy Secretary and the Under Secretary. I asked them how they would react, if in the event of a hypothetical conquest of India, while their pay got protected, they might be graded as Section Officers or Assistants. They agreed to this point. I wrote out a long note to the minister (Mrs Indira Gandhi) setting forth the whole case with a recommendation that the original grading might be set aside, and that he be graded one place higher, and also to disregard the adverse character roll entries and promote him to the next grade. Mrs Gandhi, who was singularly free from red tape, and had a wide and human outlook, agreed. Thus the injustice was undone.

13

These memories would not be complete unless I write about my association with Indira Gandhi when I was Joint Secretary, Ministry of Information and Broadcasting. She joined as minister in July 1964, and I was appointed Joint Secretary in October 1964. I had a close association with her till January 1966, when she became Prime Minister. Others close to her as Prime Minister have written ably about her, and I claim no competition with them. My role is humbler. I knew her when she put on the ministerial mantle as a young woman and fresh to the task. My observations are those of one who claims to have had her confidence at the time.

In 1964-65, Indira Gandhi was still at once the daughter of her mother and father. She had all the gentleness and grace and even shyness of her mother. Her large eyes sparkled with quietness and serenity. But there was also the scintillating intelligence of her father shining out of her eyes and face. She had a neatness about her dress and bearing. Like Panditji, she could smile at a repartee or an intelligent remark.

She liked things tidy and well-arranged about her and appreciated orderliness and flowers and flower arrangements. According to her taste, flowers and planters were put by me downstairs from where she climbed into the lift for her first-floor office in North Block. A flower arrangement at her table delighted her.

She was artistic by temperament and inclination, an instinct inherited from both her parents. Even while talking, she would make small drawings of birds or trees or animals on paper. I had collected quite a number of them. They were finely drawn and showed her artistic instinct. She asked me once why I collected them, and I told her they were pieces of art. These drawings show a delicacy which a person of artistic leanings alone can make. In any case she made these sketches like a girl in school, while the teacher is delivering a puerile lecture.

Her table was without files and neat when one went to see her, giving the visitor an impression that she had nothing on her mind and was free to receive the visitor and their problems.

Another characteristic of Mrs Gandhi was her shyness and reluctance to make speeches or talk as political leaders do. In this she was very much like her mother, frugal of word and speech except to the extent necessary. I am grateful for her confidence in me, and her permitting me to speak at the Consultative Committee meetings for her or taking me to the cabinet meetings along with her. This was also partly due to her reluctance to make speeches or elaborate to unnecessary lengths. But when she spoke, she did so with vehemence and determination and with her father's dignity. While speaking on the Madras immolations in Parliament, when the ministry was accused of having issued a circular in Hindi, she did so with indignant righteousness, and it was a great speech.

She rarely took a very academic view of issues, and was unfettered by bureaucratic red tape. Her decisions were speedy. She was also in the habit of correcting drafts put up by senior officers. She told me once not to get discouraged by this, as it did not reflect on my writing skills but that it was her habit. In the ministry I found her extremely sympathetic to staff needs, especially to the needs of the artists of AIR.

When Parliament was in session, she would sit in her room in Parliament House for part of the day, as did the other Union ministers. One of the problems facing the I&B Ministry was to get a suitable site for the Delhi TV station. She asked me to come with her to the Minister of Works and Housing while they were in Parliament House. We started together for the room of the minister that was exactly on the other side of Parliament House. The Rajya Sabha was not in session. So instead of going round the entire semicircle, she took a direct route across the Rajya Sabha House which was empty. But a tall Sikh marshal was standing guard at the door. I was following her with the file of the case. She entered the hall and had gone halfway, when looking back she noticed that I had been stopped by the marshal. While as an MP she could go across, I could not, under the rules of the Parliament, even when the Rajya Sabha was not in session and the hall was empty. So she came back, caught hold of my hand like a playful girl, asked the marshal to look the other way and we ran together hand in hand across the house, while the marshal looked away all the time. Mrs Gandhi retained a girlish, playful temperament even when serious affairs faced her. In any case, she still had it in 1965-66, before she became the Prime Minister and heavier responsibilities weighed her down and made her temperamentally sour, especially at the time of the great Congress divide of 1969.

Another incident relates to an I&B Ministry lunch which all the officials of the ministry hosted annually. In 1965, they hosted it in Lodi Gardens and invited the minister also. It was a Sunday. When I reached, Mrs Gandhi arrived in her private car driven by her son Sanjay Gandhi. So we walked in together. At a point where the pathway forked, she asked me which way to go and I pointed left. I did it on pure instinct. As Joint Secretary Administration I should have been sure. She perhaps noticed some hesitation on my mind, and asked if I was sure of the way, and was I misleading her. I replied I could never mislead her. A little while later all the staff were sighted and the direction we were going in turned out to be the correct one. I heaved a sigh of relief. She sat with the entire staff, and though her own lunch was meager, she urged Sanjay to have his fill.

In 1965 I had issued a series of transfer orders of officers belonging to the Central Information Service. One Mr Srinivasan who was in the News Division of AIR, was, for certain reasons, transferred to the Publications Division. Being politically strong, he refused to take the orders. Mr Pattabhiraman, who was Deputy Minister I&B, told me that on a recommendation, the minister, Mrs Gandhi, had cancelled the transfer. However, I made out a case for enforcing the transfer orders, and placing Srinivasan under suspension. I took it personally to her. She looked at me and then signed the note. It however became unnecessary to enforce it, as Srinivasan, having been told about the impending suspension, joined his new assignment immediately.

When I joined the ministry, the question of installing 1000 KW medium wave transmitters had been discussed for some years. We had not been able to do it because of international regulations, though every other country had installed it. China was beaming signals at the border with 500 to 1000 KW transmitters. So I spoke to Mrs Gandhi that the practical decision would be that we also followed suit. She agreed at once and directed me to go ahead, which I did. She wasted no time on nonsense and red tape.

Another time, Mr Jha, the Secretary, had taken a file to her and she had rejected the proposal. The Cabinet Secretary directed me to take it again to the minister for approval. I studied the file and took it to Mrs Gandhi. She was working and asked me what the matter was. I told her that I had brought the file of the case she had rejected. She said her decision remained as before and returned to her work. After a few minutes she looked up at me and repeated that once she had disagreed, she would never agree. I said I had made a note of that but kept sitting. After some time she again looked at me and said that she did not agree with her father mostly, or even with her grandfather. In fact, she had not agreed with Gandhiji too sometimes, and all of them had always told her that she was in the right in those matters. I smiled knowingly and laughed, at which she looked at me and asked why I had laughed. I told her that for some months now I had been trying to figure out the secret of her obstinacy and that now it had been revealed to me. She broke into a laugh. Then she asked me what I wanted her to do about the file. I told her that I had studied the file and the proposal was in our interest. She immediately signed it.

This was Indira Gandhi in my time. She needed deep loyalty and also confidence that what was being proposed to her had been properly looked at from her angle. If this exceptionally intelligent, shy and graceful woman turned harsher and more wary subsequently it was because of the great spilt of 1969 when she had to fight for her survival. She was earthy, and yet there was something ethereal about her. So far as I am concerned, I consider it a glorious association in my career.

There are however, one or two things which I must mention. As far as my impression goes, she did not have much regard for Lal Bahadur Shastri as Prime Minister. His style of functioning was not to her liking. She told me once that Shastriji had no method or system, and that even she as minister had to wait for two hours without meeting him, and that all sorts of people at all time had access to him which made serious consultation impossible. In 1965, when the UPSC turned down the proposal to appoint Dr Narayan Menon as DG, AIR, she asked me to nevertheless issue orders appointing him immediately, which I did. When the proposal was referred to the Appointment Committee of the Cabinet, Shastriji wrote strongly against this appointment and directed that this be cancelled forthwith. She did not do it and disregarded it, till we found another way of appointing him to the post after a few months.

She did not consider Shastriji fit to put on the mantle of her illustrious father. Despite all her socialistic claims, Mrs Gandhi had an inbred aristocracy in her. Pandit Nehru himself had a privileged upbringing and was always elevated to the highest positions. Mrs Gandhi, too, by birth and upbringing, stood on an aristocratic pedestal, and she regarded the smaller men around her as mere plebians, viewing them with something bordering on contempt. As Shastriji died within two years of Nehru's death, the Nehru atmosphere still held sway when Indira Gandhi assumed the reins of government as Prime Minister. It has been stated by some eminent journalist close to Shastriji that the latter had mentioned to him that if he lived four more years, Y.B. Chavan would be the Prime Minister and that if he lived only two years, Mrs Gandhi would be the next Prime Minister.

There is one case worth mentioning which shows Mrs Gandhi had a tilt towards the Soviet Union. We had to buy a 1000 KW transmitter. Yugoslavia had submitted a tender for a tropicalised unit, the parts of which were available anywhere in the world. The Russians did not give a tender. They wanted their unit to be purchased by negotiation. Mrs Gandhi asked me to ensure its purchase in consultation with our counsel in Moscow, and not to go in for the Yugoslav transmitter. The cost came to about rupees one crore.

In order to make sure that the transmitter was of the desired quality, I directed the Chief Engineer of AIR to go to Moscow and see its functioning. I also told him to go to Belgrade and study the other transmitter. He came back and gave a detailed technical report in which he reported that the Russian transmitter was a sturdy but an outdated one, and we would be forever dependent on them for parts. He therefore made a recommendation that this be rejected in favour of the Yugoslavian transmitter. I agreed with him and submitted a note to Mrs Gandhi. She wrote only one sentence in her order, that we would go in for the Russian transmitter. I, however, persuaded her to buy the Yugoslavian transmitter also, which got installed. I negotiated with the Russians and got a clause inserted in the agreement for supply of parts to last five years. This transmitter was also installed. This incident showed a leaning towards the Soviet Union at the time that the non-alignment policy of Pandit Nehru was given a definite slant towards the Soviet.

But despite all this, she stands out for me as a lovable personality. There was something fascinating about her. Born and bred in an illustrious house of culture and urbanity, she was in a class apart, intellectually and emotionally too. During the Janata regime they forgot the sacrifices of her family and her own, and deprived her of her earned seat in Parliament and put her in jail. But the masses felt differently despite all the wild outcries against her in Delhi.

There are a few more memories worth mentioning. One is the introduction of commercial broadcasting on All India Radio. While Indira Gandhi was the minister, she parried questions on the subject and had not made up her mind whether or not it should be introduced. But Raj Bahadurji, who succeeded her as minister, felt that it should be introduced. The DG of AIR opposed it. Even the directors of the BBC and Canadian broadcasting organizations met me and begged me to save AIR which had a unique reputation in the world, from commercializing itself. I wrote out one of my notes on the subject agreeing with the DG. The Secretary of the ministry, Ashok Mitra, also wrote a fine essay on the subject opposing the introduction of commercial broadcasting. Raj Bahadur, an able lawyer of repute, however, in a more than sixteen-page note, said why he disagreed with us. I met the minister and asked him whether he would permit me to answer the points raised by him. He felt that enough had been said and now the orders should be implemented. So, true to the traditions of the service, I prepared a note for the Cabinet, recommending the introduction of commercial broadcasting on AIR. It was introduced some time in 1967-68. The good and bad effects are already to be seen. It may be mentioned here that Raj Bahadurji was a great minister. He was responsible for the AIR station at Mathura.

The other important item then taken up was a recommendation of the A.K. Chanda Committee on broadcasting, that AIR be converted into an autonomous corporation. A learned note on the subject was written by A.K. Sen, later DG, AIR, opposing the proposition as impracticle and pernicious. I also wrote out an exhaustive note with cogent reasons agreeing with A.K. Sen. The Secretary of the Ministry Ashok Mitra also wrote opposing it. The minister agreed and the matter was dropped. And yet without studying the file and weighing the pros and cons, the Janata government in 1977 appointed the Verghese Committee on the subject. The recommendations made were a product of ignorance and false notions of autonomy in our country. I wrote to L.K. Advani, the then minister, drawing his attention to the file on the subject. Later, learning more by experience than advice, they went slow and dropped the matter. Sardar Patel, however, was forthright in 1950, when he stated in Parliament that the government, elected by the majority of people and representing the majority in Parliament, has a right to voice its point of view on AIR, and reach the masses according to the programme and policy of the government.

An account of the I&B Ministry would not be complete without mention of Nandini Satpathy, who was Deputy Minister in 1966-68. She was a young lady of great merit and integrity. Her deep dark eyes shone with child-like simplicity and sincerity and she was always true to her word and in her intentions. She was meant more for higher ideals of life than for the polluting atmosphere of politics. Yet she lent grace, charm and integrity to mundane matters of administration. She was an artist by temperament, and was greatly in favour of bettering the lot of the staff artists of AIR. She was also a great votary for the Mother of Pondicherry. She was a rare person whom fate and circumstances persecuted relentlessly. In my opinion she was certainly not cut out for the rough and tumble of the crafty and devious job of a Chief Minister. Not once while she was my minister, did she ask me to do anything dubious or unbecoming. She was always for keeping things straightforward.

I visited Bhubaneshwar and Cuttack in June 1968 for a week at her behest to straighten out outstanding problems of the Cuttack radio station. We were also sent by plane to Jeypore in district Koraput, a godforsaken place, where the source of drinking water was a big pond. The hillocks around were barren and radiated heat in the summer in June. From the height of Koraput district (where we stayed the night in the Inspection House) one could see for miles around, the sun-parched, desolate countryside covered with dry forests and small hillocks. There were no railway lines and the entire area was inaccessible. But it attracted the benign attention of Nandiniji. In Orissa I found her to be absolutely carefree. I particularly marked the girlish delight on her face as she moved about freely in Cuttack and Puri, away from the tensions of North Block in New Delhi.

It may be of interest here to record something about the Public Accounts Committee (PAC) which used to meet every year to call upon each ministry to explain the audit objections that had been raised. The Public Accounts Committee consists of Members of Parliament, mostly of the Opposition. The intention behind the committee is to allow representatives of the Parliament to look into the working of the executive, especially where finances are concerned. What actually happens is that the Auditor General sits along with the Chairman and the members, and the Secretary of the ministry and the officers are called upon to explain the objections raised by the audit party. Matters relate to a period for which sometimes no secretary or officer present at the PAC is responsible. So they answer for the actions of their predecessors and are very often unable to recall why a particular action was taken or not taken under the circumstances then prevailing, except on the basis of what is recorded on the file. And for this the present Secretary and the officers are taken to task. During the sessions of these committees, I noticed that the main aim of individual members of the Committee was often not to grasp the explanations but to show off their importance by using foul and unbecoming language towards the officers for acts for which they were not responsible or which they did for perfectly good reasons that were not understood by the MP. Nothing pleased an MP more than reprimanding the highest officers in the presence of his kinsmen or his party men to show off his authority. The secretaries and the departmental officers could not join issue as protestations could amount to contempt of Parliament.

I faced several sessions of the Public Accounts Committee. Once in 1965 with A.N. Jha, Secretary, and another time when Jha was on leave, as in-charge of the Ministry of I&B. I recall one instance when Mr Jha was conducting the ceremony and facing the never to be satisfied members of the PAC. The session had lasted more than two or three hours, and we had answered and answered. Then came up a case of the Publications Division. Despite the explanations given by Mr Jha, the members would not be satisfied. So Mr Jha drew upon the ultimate weapon in his armoury. He called upon Mohan Rao, Director of the Publications Division, to reply. Now Mr Mohan Rao, an erudite scholar, and a most competent officer, had the habit of speaking on and on, without a comma, semi-colon, or full stop, in sheer disregard of the other party and without taking notice of reactions on the other side. He got up and spoke and spoke and spoke, totally unmindful of interruptions from members of the PAC till the latter got fed up, and told Secretary Jha that they were satisfied and the session was over.

I must not forget to make a mention of Rafi Ahmad Kidwai, the great political leader of the Independence movement. He was Home Minister in UP in 1946-47, and Communications and later Food Minister of the Union Government. I met him once in UP in February 1947, when having been unfairly treated by the government, I hurled impertinences at him, and he bore it most coolly. He was the man who made resources available when Kashmir was in danger in 1947-48. He was the man who alone could scrap the food control and rationing schemes, which clutched the country's neck like the fabled old man of the sea. I attended one of the shortest meetings in the Food and Agriculture Ministry in 1953, when he stated his point of view and terminated the meeting, overruling G.L. Nanda and others of the Planning Commission.

It was his custom to enquire at the time of dinner whether any person in the compound of 6, King Edward Road (now Maulana Azad Road), was without food. He had helped hundreds of people big and small. Princes were as much at home with him as the smallest and the humblest. His home was the home of anybody who needed help. Once an old-time peon of his came to him, and managed to obtain a cheque of Rs 3000 from him, for the marriage of his daughter. When the man was gone, his orderlies informed Kidwai Saheb that the man had no daughter. To this Kidwai Saheb made a typical reply. He said that the poor man was perhaps in some unfortunate situation that he had to invent a lie.

He was always kind to me, and commanded loyalty from all those he came across. I did not terminate the services of an employee in the Indian Airlines despite his culpable conduct, simply because Kidwai Saheb had had him employed, and I could not do him harm after Kidwai Saheb's death. Hundreds of Hindu and Muslim girls were married with Kidwai Saheb's assistance. The mahant of Gorakhnath Temple, Digvijai Nath, President of the Hindu Mahasabha, who raised a hue and cry against Kidwai Saheb in 1946, told me that the largest and most frequent help he had received personally and financially, was from Kidwai Saheb. Even today, hundreds of poor people go to his mazaar in village Masauli in Barabanki district and make offerings and prayers. He was a saint in disguise. It is a pity that no biography of this man of the masses of India has yet been written.

14

Towards the end of 1968, I was overtaken by great misfortune. My elder son Arvind lost his wife, a girl hardly twenty-four years old. My second son fell gravely ill. I was shattered physically, and mentally I was in ruins. I came to the Board of Revenue in Allahabad. I had left Allahabad in 1936, and the wheel having turned full circle, I was back at the confluence of the Ganga and Yamuna. Here my mental equilibrium was restored and my son recovered as well.

I have continued to stay at Allahabad where I have retreated from the tensions of Delhi, and where the atmosphere is peaceful and homely. Time does not fly here and one can stop and ponder. The rush of life is missing. The annual Magh Mela and the Kumbh and Ardh Kumbh melas on the banks of the Ganga are unrivalled. A congregation of millions of men and women from all over the country and even countries outside India flock to this mela where a city in tents goes up. There are lights in the evening on the vast bank competing with the stars, as the waters of the Ganga and Yamuna sparkle and glisten amidst the musical rippling of waves. Apart from the vast concourse of humanity, religious teachers and saints from all over India and the interior abodes of Himalaya come to pay homage to the river Ganga. It is a sight to see the huge concourse of multicoloured humanity moving towards the confluence with the single-minded objective of taking a bath. For thousands of years this sea of humanity has converged at Allahabad. The confluence of the olive-green waters of the Ganga and the dark waters of the Yamuna has been described and praised in inimitable verses by Kalidas.

Allahabad or Prayag is also known as Tirtha Raj. It is a great satisfaction to come in the evening of one's life here, from the temporal capital Delhi to the spiritual capital Prayag.

Thus ends my story. As I stand in the evening of my life, in the peaceful surroundings of Allahabad, I have no regrets and feel so grateful for a fulsome career.

As I sit in contemplation and look back, faces and scenes light up in my mind's eye, and pass through the stage in a silent procession. My eyes are moist that many faces which I have seen laughing and full of life are no more.

Like a mountain around which streams and rivulets emerge and rush forth into the ocean beyond, like that misty mountain I stand, look back, and with wistful eyes remember.

EPILOGUE

This memoir covers the period till 1971 when I retired from service. Though I live in Allahabad now*, I occasionally go to Delhi to see the changes that have been wrought on the fair face of the country's capital. Much has happened during these years. A great many faces mentioned in these memories have vanished. Dr A.N. Jha is gone. He began gloriously at Allahabad University where his father Dr Ganganath Jha was the Vice Chancellor. Having had a brilliant career as Secretary, Ministry of Information and Broadcasting and finally as Lt. Governor of Delhi, he died prematurely at Raj Bhawan, Delhi. He was of large build, in proportion to his magnanimous nature and kindly disposition. He was the kind of man about whom Shakespeare said Nature might stand up and say: here was a man.

---

*This Epilogue was written sometime in 1981.

Josh Malihabadi died in Pakistan, on alien soil. His death was not noticed much in Pakistan. He always regretted having migrated to Pakistan and told me so when I met him in Karachi.

Closely following him came Firaq Saheb, or Raghupati Sahai, my teacher in BA 1st year. I met Firaq Saheb, a giant in the field of literature, several times in Allahabad. He was keen to dispose of his manuscripts to the government at a reasonable price. Though over eighty and almost incapacitated, his eyes were keen and his brain intact. He was cremated by the River Ganga and I had the privilege of being present.

R.P. Bhargava of the ICS who had been so close to me since Pilibhit days is no more. Gone too is Krishan Chand, who became Lt. Governor of Delhi, whom I had known since 1946. Many other faces of relations and friends with whom I have lived and laughed are no more. The hand of death has been unmerciful and unrelenting.

During these years, I have been particularly obsessed by the ephemeral nature of all matter and of life. Each moment, this body is dying and decaying. In this eternal process of decay and destruction, childhood, youth and old age are but stages or milestones. One is reminded of the reply given by Yudhishthira to the Yaksha in the *Mahabharata* that death is the churning of all creatures and matter in a hot cauldron beneath which the sun is burning like firewood. And unless you have faith in your Maker, it all seems so futile.

During these years I have seen the decay of moral standards. The materialism of the West has overtaken us, and traditions and values are fast crumbling. Men and women, torn away from old moorings, hang between earth and sky, uprooted with nothing to hold on to, while the Western world is going crazy over our saffron-clad sadhus in search of peace. But meanwhile our sadhus have fallen for the lure of the West. They are either in search of foreign disciples or migrating to the States or Canada. I have heard some of them saying that the rich Americans are godlier. Undoubtedly, 'All virtues dwell where gold is' and all this degeneration in public life has led to a scramble for wealth and inevitable corruption. Distrust is now the hallmark of nations and of individuals.

On the political stage, the era of greatness appears to have gone. All the Chief Ministers, except those of West Bengal and Tamil Nadu, are small men of no consequence. These weaklings are agents and mouthpieces of the Centre. The federal element in our Constitution has yielded to the unitary concept in practice. In these times of speed and lawlessness and industrially underdeveloped conditions, and the confusions generated by overpopulation and poverty, it appears to many that only a dictatorship can act and deliver. I see the age of dictatorship arriving at our doorstep gradually but surely. In fact, with Mrs Gandhi at the helm, it is almost here, wearing the false apparel and trappings of democracy. It is fortunate that bred in the best traditions of the Nehru family, she is a benign dictator. I wonder what the future holds for our country.

The trends across the world are forebodings of a catastrophe. Man is more engrossed in manufacturing weapons of destruction than in alleviating misery and suffering. These trends have to be arrested. In my opinion it is only India which can show the way. As the land of Buddha, Gandhi and Swami Vivekanand, we have shown that spirit can triumph over matter. With the resurgence of fundamentalism, there has to be a resurgence of the spirit according to our Indian traditions. We have to go back to simplicity and the Upanishads. Then alone can we halt the pace of destruction and open an era of spiritual peace, which encompasses all understanding.

It will be pertinent to quote Dr Amarnath Jha, the great Vice Chancellor of the Allahabad University, who wrote in 1951: 'Everyone speaks of spiritualism of the East. Some in tones of contempt, others in a spirit of uninformed wonder. It seems paradoxical that the land where lofty ideas were enunciated and the highest points of metaphysical speculation reached, should be regarded as being underdeveloped. The explanation of the paradox is that a country is judged today by purely material standards. The extent of industrialization, the abundance of mechanical devices and technical skill stand for progress: It is the advance made in nuclear weapons, in space flying or in other feats by scientists in harnessing matter for purposes of destruction or material comforts that make a nation advanced and great. But they are leading mankind to disaster and to unending unhappiness and disturbance of the spirit. Even today our great teachers have called you back to hearken to the ultimate truth of the Gita and the Upanishad. The whole of West stricken with a paralysis of materialism is looking to our country for peace, for sustenance of their disturbed soul.'

I have digressed in the dissertations above from the spirit of memoirs. Here in Allahabad now the Muir Hostel boys and teachers have several times invited me as an old inmate to come and speak. Many of my old departmental people from All India Radio, Excise Department and Indian Airlines come and meet me. People from my village in Faizabad come for help and I render what I can. And thus life goes on for me here, steeped in my books of literature in English, Hindi and Sanskrit. The *Bhagwat*, the *Ramayana*, the *Mahabharata* and the Upanishads interest me more and more. And I now feel as Tennyson felt in his poem:

Sunset and evening star,
    And one clear call for me!
And may there be no moaning of the bar,
    When I put out to sea,

But such a tide as moving seems asleep,
    Too full for sound and foam,
When that which drew from out the boundless deep
    Turns again home.

ALSO FROM SPEAKING TIGER

IN THE SERVICE OF FREE INDIA
B.D. Pande

'[B.D. Pande's] memoirs, written largely by hand, in 1986, two years after he demitted his last government assignment, carried his instructions that they should not be published [till]...five years after his death. B.D. Pande died in 2009. His daughter Ratna Sudarshan has painstakingly edited and published the memoirs in 2021...Present and future generations must be grateful to her for making available within the covers of this book an insider's perceptive account of economic and political developments in India in her first four decades after independence.'

—*The Indian Express*

In the decades following 1947, as the tallest national leaders were building a new India, they were supported by a band of remarkable, idealistic civil servants. Among these officers was Bhairab Datt Pande, a young man from the Himalayan district of Kumaon, who joined the Indian Civil Service in 1939. Over 40 years as civil servant, and later as governor, he played an important role in the country's administration, and interacted with leaders like Indira Gandhi (as cabinet secretary during the Emergency), Morarji Desai and Jyoti Basu. His memoir—which, respecting his wish, has been published posthumously—is a fascinating record of his own life and that of India in the half century after Independence.

Pande chronicles several landmark events and initiatives that he either participated in or witnessed. As food commissioner of Bihar in the early 1950s, he helped increase food-grain allotment to the state and drew up a new famine code. His work in the Community Development programme still has important lessons for today's Panchayati Raj institutions. After retirement, he was governor of West Bengal during the resurgence of Naxalism in the early 1980s, and of Punjab in 1983-84—a tragic and turbulent year in the history of the state and the nation. His compelling narration of the behind-the-scenes events and negotiations leading up to the Anandpur Sahib Resolution and Operation Bluestar is of great value.

www.ingramcontent.com/pod-product-compliance
Lightning Source LLC
LaVergne TN
LVHW041941070526
838199LV00051BA/2863